Find

Peace

in

Advent!

"Gary Zimak's gift is to bring people, through scripture reading and reflection, to the peace that only Jesus can give. With this little Advent book, Zimak does it again. Take a few minutes a day to read *Find Peace in Advent!* and, as Christmas approaches, come close to the one who can truly give you rest."

Cy Kellett
Host of *Catholic Answers Live*

"Gary Zimak intuitively crafts an immersive Advent journey with *Find Peace in Advent!* His 'read, reflect, respond, pray' process fosters an engaging experience that feels not only accessible but tangible."

Regina Boyd
Therapist and author of *Leaving Loneliness Behind*

"Gary Zimak has done it again! Weaving his own experiences into reflection and prayer, he gives us the opportunity to more fully enter into the season. It can be tough to find peace at any time, but especially during Advent—or 'the holidays' as we know it now. But with God—and a little help from Zimak—it can be done!"

Gus Lloyd
Host of *Seize the Day* on Sirius XM's The Catholic Channel

Find Peace in Advent!

4 WEEKS TO WORRYING LESS AT CHRISTMAS

GARY ZIMAK

AVE MARIA PRESS AVE Notre Dame, Indiana

Founded in 1865, Ave Maria Press is a ministry of the United States Province of Holy Cross.

www.avemariapress.com

Paperback: ISBN-13 978-1-64680-291-3

E-book: ISBN-13 978-1-64680-292-0

Cover image © Gettyimages.com.

Cover and text design by Brian C. Conley.

Printed and bound in the United States of America.

Library of Congress Cataloging-in-Publication Data is available.

Contents

Introduction

Is it really possible to find peace during one of the busiest and stress-filled times of the year? If you posed the question to those frantically trying to survive the pre-Christmas rat race, many would answer with a resounding no. Judging from the title of this book, however, you undoubtedly realize that I disagree. Not only do I believe it's possible to find peace during the hectic four weeks leading up to Christmas, but also I will show you how. All it takes is a few minutes a day and your willingness to follow the lead of the Holy Spirit. Before we get to the specifics, however, let's discuss one of the most misunderstood and underappreciated seasons of the year: Advent.

At some point during my twelve years of Catholic education, I learned that Lent and Advent were special seasons in the Church year. While I can't pinpoint the exact moment, I do know that I grasped this message in the first few years of grade school. It didn't take long for Lent to become more important and practical than Advent to me. After all, everyone knows that Catholics should give up something for Lent. Advent was sort of a mystery. I knew I was supposed to prepare for the birth of Jesus, but hadn't he already been born two thousand years ago? It's no wonder that, for me and many others, Advent simply becomes a four-week waiting period for Christmas.

Somewhere along the way, I became intrigued by the concept of Advent. I knew it was about waiting and preparation, but how could I wait for an event that already took place—and how should I be preparing? Upon consulting the *Catechism of the Catholic Church* (524), this is what I found:

> When the Church celebrates the liturgy of Advent each year, she makes present this ancient expectancy of the Messiah, for by sharing in the long preparation for the Savior's first coming, the faithful renew their ardent desire for his second coming. By celebrating the precursor's birth and martyrdom, the Church unites herself to his desire: "He must increase, but I must decrease."

Okay, now it started to make a little more sense to me. By tapping into the expectation felt by those who originally waited for the birth of the Messiah, I can anticipate his Second Coming. While this definitely helped me to better understand the part about waiting for an event that already took place (the birth of the Messiah), it didn't help me to actually care more about his Second Coming. Like many others, I was caught up in struggling to believe that Jesus would be returning anytime soon. After all, if it hasn't happened in two thousand years, why should I expect it to happen in my lifetime?

Although the Advent mystery was becoming clearer, there were still two nagging questions in my mind. What should I do to prepare for the next coming of Jesus? And how can I view that event with a greater sense of urgency? The *Catechism* does a nice job of answering the first question by referring to the life of the precursor (John the Baptist) and his belief that he must decrease and Jesus must increase. For Jesus to increase in me, I need to give him some room to work. At the end of Advent, my life should reflect more of Jesus and less of me. But what exactly does that mean?

"Less of me" means not less of my personality and unique characteristics but rather less of my sinfulness and imperfections. For that to happen, I need to make room for Jesus and invite him to live more fully in me. That's the preparation I should be doing during Advent. St. Paul sums it up perfectly when he writes, "It is no longer I who live, but Christ who lives in me" (Gal 2:20, RSVCE). By the end of Advent, I should resemble Jesus more than I did four weeks earlier.

Now that I understand the goal of Advent, what can I do to increase my expectation for the Lord's Second Coming? Let's be totally honest with one another: very few of us expect Jesus to come in glory anytime soon. It absolutely can happen, but it's hard to become emotionally invested in that expectation. One way to increase our sense of urgency about meeting Jesus is to focus on the hour of our death. While that can make our encounter with the Lord more imminent, it can't be counted on to move us to action today. After all, most of us don't really expect to die in the next few weeks. Setting our sights on Christmas Day, on the other hand, is a total game changer.

After reflecting on this for a while, it occurred to me that there's a simple solution, and it has to do with something that's on our minds throughout the Advent season: Christmas! Even if we don't expect to die or for Jesus to come in glory anytime soon, we all know that Christmas Day (and Jesus) will arrive on December 25. That gives us four weeks to prepare to meet him—either in his Second Coming or when we die—by becoming more like him. Four weeks is doable. We don't know when he will come again, but we do know we have the opportunity to meet the Lord when he comes to us in our everyday lives. Advent is our chance to sharpen our focus on that encounter. Looking at it that way is great motivation for making every day count!

THIS BOOK

Little by little, my Advent discoveries began to make their way into my personal devotions and proved to be effective. Excited by the idea of Advent becoming a fruitful season in my life, I began to share my thoughts in radio interviews and blog posts. Eventually, I got a strong feeling that I was supposed to write a book on the subject. It was the same feeling I got a few years ago when my book *Give Up Worry for Lent!* was conceived. I took the feeling very seriously, but I wasn't clear on the format of the new book. That all changed one day while, in the middle of my morning prayers, the thought came to me that there should really be a *Give Up Worry for Lent!* written for Advent. Almost immediately after getting that thought, a title popped into my mind: *Finding Peace in Advent*. The vision was beginning to come alive, and this book was becoming a reality.

In *Give Up Worry for Lent!*, I discovered a formula that has proven to be successful year after year. Catholics look for something to give up for Lent but often feel obligated to make it as painful as possible. As a result, the lasting benefit of Lenten sacrifice becomes overshadowed by a "this has to hurt" philosophy, which often leads to abandoning the whole process. *Give Up Worry for Lent!* is attractive primarily because of a paradigm shift. It replaces the typical "grin and bear it" Lenten approach with a less painful (but highly effective) method that not only draws the reader closer to God but also offers the promise of peace.

Find Peace in Advent! builds on the success of *Give Up Worry for Lent!* and moves its proven technique into the Advent season. In addition to the promise of peace during one of the least peaceful times of the year, this book will relieve you of the burden of coming up with a practical Advent program. The daily readings and reflections are easy to digest and tie in to the daily Mass readings and the rhythm of the Advent season.

You're probably wondering how this book will deliver peace, especially in the four activity-filled weeks leading up to Christmas. It's a great question and one that needs to be addressed. Each day's material includes a Bible verse and a prayer, which means you will come in direct contact with God whenever you open up this book. By listening to the Lord's words in scripture and conversing with him in prayer, peace will flow organically. To put it simply, something always happens when we seek God in prayer and scripture. More often than not, peace is the first "something" produced by that meeting.

HOW IT WORKS

Find Peace in Advent! consists of a series of daily entries, beginning with the First Sunday of Advent and continuing through Christmas Day. Designed to be read in five minutes or less, each daily entry is made up of four parts:

- Read: a Bible verse taken from the daily Mass readings
- Reflect: a short reflection based on the Bible verse

- Respond: a suggested call to action based on the Bible verse
- Pray: a short prayer that puts you in touch with Jesus

This method is so practical and doable that it will fit into even the busiest person's schedule. If it sounds simple, that's because it is. As with so many spiritual exercises, however, its simplicity doesn't make it ineffective. In other words, it works!

Throughout the liturgical year (or Church year), the Sunday Mass readings rotate on a three-year cycle (A, B, and C). For this reason, I have included reflections for all three cycles of Sunday Advent readings. Only one cycle is used during the weekdays of Advent, however, so those readings don't change year to year. (If you're unsure of the rhythms of the current liturgical year, the United States Conference of Catholic Bishops offers a liturgical calendar online at https://www.usccb.org/committees/divine-worship/liturgical-calendar.)

While the layout of this book is relatively straightforward, there are a few things to keep in mind. When we reach December 17 (regardless of which day of the week it falls on), the Church enters a special, final phase of Advent preparations with its own unique set of readings. Therefore, you'll see a note after the Sunday readings of the third week of Advent alerting you to this fact. Once you reach December 17, all remaining Advent weekday reflections will appear in the section "Weekdays of Advent: December 17–24" starting on page 99.

December 8 is always the solemnity of the Immaculate Conception of the Blessed Virgin Mary, so when you reach that date, turn to page 96 for a special reflection.

By turning the page and moving into the reflections, you'll begin an Advent journey designed to draw you closer to Jesus.

This "one day at a time" journey will also deliver the peace that "surpasses all understanding" (Phil 4:7). Know that I'll be traveling with you—and so will the Holy Spirit. We'll work together to prepare you to welcome Jesus more fully into your life on Christmas Day. Oh, and by the way, you won't have to wait until Christmas to experience the peace that the Lord brings. You'll begin feeling it as soon as the journey begins.

So what do you think? Ready to get started? As I write this, I'm praying that the next four weeks will bear an abundance of good fruit in your life and that you'll grow closer to Jesus than ever before. Thanks for traveling with me. Here we go!

Jesus Is Coming. Let's Get Ready!

First Sunday of Advent
YEAR A

First Reading: Isaiah 2:1–5
Responsorial Psalm: Psalm 122:1–2, 3–4, 4–5, 6–7, 8–9
Second Reading: Romans 13:11–14
Gospel: Matthew 24:37–44

READ

> It is the hour now for you to awake from sleep.
> For our salvation is nearer now than when we first
> believed; the night is advanced, the day is at hand.
> Let us then throw off the works of darkness [and]
> put on the armor of light.
>
> —Romans 13:11–12

REFLECT

Today, we begin the season of preparation known as Advent. It's a time set aside for preparing to welcome Jesus—when he comes again in glory, when we die, or on Christmas Day, whichever comes first. The date of the meeting doesn't really matter, as long as we're prepared when it happens. So, how should we prepare? Cleaning up our internal clutter and making room for Jesus is a great place to start.

Advent is here, and we're closer than ever before to that meeting with Jesus. As we discussed in the introduction, however, we'll temporarily put aside trying to determine which kind of meeting we'll be having and focus on his arrival on Christmas

Day. That way, if any of those other two events take place before Christmas, we'll still be ready!

Let's take Paul's advice and "awake from sleep" by resolving to make this a fruitful Advent. As with anything else in life, we'll get out of Advent what we put into it. If we work on making room for Jesus every day, our efforts will be rewarded and we'll celebrate Christmas closer to him than we are now. With the help of the Holy Spirit, we'll seek to identify anything that pulls us away from Jesus and take concrete steps to make any necessary changes.

Ultimately, how much we progress we make will be up to the Holy Spirit. Our goal is simply to do our best and let the Holy Spirit do the rest. Trying to move too fast or control the outcome will bring us only frustration. On the other hand, following the lead of the Spirit will not only be effective but also result in the supernatural peace that "surpasses all understanding" (Phil 4:7).

RESPOND

Congratulations! By reading this reflection, you've taken the first step in responding to Paul's instruction to "awake from sleep." There will be more steps ahead, but this is a critical one. Many Christians never muster up the strength to enter into a meaningful Advent journey. By taking this initial step, you are on your way to "throwing off the works of darkness and putting on the armor of light." Today, let's commit to take one step each day for the duration of Advent, as we prepare to welcome Jesus.

PRAY

Dear Jesus, thank you for your willingness to enter our world, even though it meant you would experience rejection, suffering, and death. I realize that you did it because you love me. While I could never pay you back fully, I want to do something. For the remainder of Advent, I'm going to work on making room for you in my life. That may cause me to leave behind some bad habits and comforts I've been clinging to. Please walk with me and grant me the grace I need to make the necessary changes. Amen.

First Sunday of Advent
YEAR B

First Reading: Isaiah 63:16b–17, 19b, 64:2–7
Responsorial Psalm: Psalm 80:2–3, 15–16, 18–19
Second Reading: 1 Corinthians 1:3–9
Gospel: Mark 13:33–37

READ

> Be watchful! Be alert! You do not know when the
> time will come.
>
> —Mark 13:33

REFLECT

While many changes have occurred in the past two thousand years, one thing that hasn't changed is our tendency to become shortsighted when it comes to spiritual matters. It's a problem now, and it was a problem when Jesus first spoke these words to his disciples. Like us, they frequently got so caught up in plea-sure-seeking and problem-solving that they failed to prepare for the next life. Totally aware of this tendency, Jesus reminded his followers of the temporary nature of their time on earth and urged them to "watch."

With these words, Jesus also urges us to be prepared. Despite our desire to be in control, none of us know how many days we have left on earth or when the Lord will come again. At the hour of our death or the Lord's Second Coming (depending on which occurs first), we will be judged and our eternal future decided. No matter how busy we are, we don't want to make the mistake of neglecting our spiritual life.

The next few weeks are going to be filled with more distractions than normal. In addition to the ordinary responsibilities of daily life, you will feel increased pressure to shop, bake, and indulge in parties and pre-Christmas activities. At times, it may feel as if you're barely keeping your head above water. In the very near future, you'll feel a strong temptation to put off the "unimportant" things and take care of the "important" matters that *must get done* before Christmas. For this reason, the Church intervenes and delivers this important reminder from Jesus, who has his own definition of what's truly important.

RESPOND

It would be unrealistic for me to advise you to drop everything and use the next four weeks solely to get your spiritual life in order. It would also be unrealistic to burden you with time-consuming spiritual exercises to add to your already-busy schedule. I do think it's entirely realistic, however, to ask you to spend a few minutes each day thinking about a Bible verse and preparing to welcome Jesus more deeply into your life. Done this way, Advent becomes a source of greater peace and not a burden.

We know that we'll meet Jesus when we die or when he comes again in glory, but let's focus on December 25 as our target date for meeting Jesus. Doing so gives us a concrete point in time to work toward, which will increase our sense of urgency. By taking away some of the mystery, we can better prepare for the Lord's arrival. Christmas Day marks our special celebration of the ways he comes to us in our here-and-now. Let's begin cleaning up our internal "house" to make extra room for him when he arrives!

PRAY

Dear Jesus, it's so easy to become distracted, especially in the days leading up to Christmas. With so much to get done and so little time to do it, I sometimes want to put off spiritual matters and concentrate on things that can be seen, felt, or tasted. Please help me prioritize my tasks according to *your* standards and grant me the grace to experience peace amid craziness. Amen.

First Sunday of Advent
YEAR C

First Reading: Jeremiah 33:14–16
Responsorial Psalm: Psalm 25:4–5, 8–9, 10, 14
Second Reading: 1 Thessalonians 3:12–4:2
Gospel: Luke 21:25–28, 34–36

READ

> Beware that your hearts do not become drowsy
> from carousing and drunkenness and the anxiet-
> ies of daily life, and that day catch you by surprise.
>
> —Luke 21:34

REFLECT

It's easy to see how carousing and drunkenness can cause one to lose sight of spiritual matters. It only makes sense that Jesus would issue a warning about these destructive practices. What's not so obvious, however, is the fact that the anxieties of daily life can have the same effect. I've lived it, and I can personally vouch for the truth of this statement. Life tends to be filled with distractions, which can easily cause us to lose sight of Jesus and eternal life. Recognizing the reality of the threat is the first step to protecting ourselves.

In addition to the distractions we face throughout the year, the next few weeks will be filled with additional opportunities to lose our spiritual focus. There will be a million things that "have to get done" before Christmas, as well as obligatory parties and school events. Even the "carousing and drunkenness" Jesus warned us about can be found with little effort. Unless we're careful, we can easily get so distracted by the whirlwind of Christmas preparation that we completely forget about the whole point of Advent.

Because the main focus of Advent is on the very real (but intangible) Second Coming of Christ, it's easy to get caught up in the material things that are going on at the same time. For that reason, the Church gives us a much-needed reminder in the Gospel from today's Mass. Recognizing that it's human nature to focus on the seen at the expense of the unseen, Jesus urges us to be careful. There will be a judgment day, and we will be held accountable for how we lived our lives. If we don't prepare now, we won't fare well when that time comes.

RESPOND

Forewarned is forearmed. This familiar proverb is a great reminder as we begin the season of Advent. In the Gospel from today's Mass, Jesus warns us against becoming spiritually drowsy as we prepare for eternal life. His words of caution can help us to prepare for the barrage of distractions we are about to experience over the next few weeks. While this knowledge alone isn't enough to prevent us from falling into the trap of worldly attractions, it's a great starting point.

In approximately four weeks, the world will celebrate the birth of Jesus on Christmas Day. While his birth happened two thousand years ago, it proves to us that God sends him into our lives every day, whether we are ready for him or not. The best way to prepare for this gift is by making room in your life for him. It's not too late to begin. We do it by resolving not to let the day catch us by surprise. The daily meditations in this book may take only a few minutes to read and ponder, but they are a powerful defense against spiritual laziness. Let's begin by turning to the Lord in prayer.

PRAY

Dear Jesus, thank you for warning me of the distractions I am about to face. Even though I want to prepare to celebrate your arrival on Christmas Day with a full heart, I know I'll be tempted to forgo my spiritual exercises. Please grant me the grace to remain faithful to my Advent preparation. I really want to make room to welcome you more deeply into my life. Amen.

Monday

FIRST WEEK OF ADVENT

Reading: Isaiah 2:1–5 (or Isaiah 4:2–6 in year A)
Responsorial Psalm: Psalm 122:1–2, 3–4b, 4cd–5, 6–7, 8–9
Gospel: Matthew 8:5–11

READ

> When Jesus heard this, he was amazed and said to
> those following him, "Amen, I say to you, in no one
> in Israel have I found such faith."
>
> —Matthew 8:10

REFLECT

Coming to Jesus on behalf of his paralyzed servant, the centurion believed that the Lord could heal by merely "saying the words." The man's belief in the power of Jesus was so strong that Jesus rejected the offer to heal the servant in person, stating that it wasn't necessary. The centurion was confident that the words of Jesus alone could bring about the healing.

I also find it interesting that Jesus was amazed by the faith possessed by the Roman centurion. This observation serves as a reminder that Jesus cares about what we say and do, especially when it comes to matters of faith. Not only does he notice, but also, as this story illustrates, he is moved—even amazed—by what he finds in us. This Gentile's faith was stronger than that of any of the Chosen People. Somehow, he managed to possess what they lacked. It's a great reminder of the fact that faith is a gift and not an entitlement. Its growth requires openness and humility, both of which must have been possessed by the powerful Roman officer.

RESPOND

How's your faith? Do you think Jesus would be impressed with what he finds in you? If you're like me and realize that your faith isn't what it could be, Advent provides a great opportunity to do something about it. Since faith is a gift, you can't manufacture it. You can, however, take steps that will allow it to grow.

One of the most productive things we can do, especially at the beginning of Advent, is to recognize our problem areas and shortcomings. If the faith of the centurion makes you uncomfortable, your Advent is already bearing good fruit! Many people go through life without making an effort to assess where they stand in their relationship with Jesus. Realizing that your faith is lacking puts you in an excellent position to do something about it.

Once we realize we're deficient in the faith department, what can we do? The first thing to do is pray for an increase in faith. Second, no matter how you feel, choose to exercise whatever faith you already have each day through prayer. Most of us have some sort of "impossible" situation that doesn't appear to be solvable. By turning to Jesus in prayer and using your faith, you're giving him the chance to perform a faith-boosting miracle. Furthermore, the mere fact that you're turning to him in prayer illustrates that you believe in his power. And while your faith may not be as strong as the centurion's, you're definitely on your way. Faith is like a muscle: the more you exercise it, the stronger it grows.

PRAY

Dear Jesus, I may not have the faith of the Roman centurion, but I definitely believe in you and your power to help me. Thank you for enabling me to see that my faith isn't as strong as it should be. It's an important lesson, but I don't think you want it to end there. I know you want me to trust you more and turn to you with confident expectation. That's the kind of faith possessed by the centurion, and it's the kind of faith I want. Please grant me the grace to believe in you more, especially when I need a miracle. One of my Advent goals is for you to be amazed at my faith too. I might have a long way to go, but I believe it's possible. Amen.

Tuesday
FIRST WEEK OF ADVENT

Reading: Isaiah 11:1–10
Responsorial Psalm: Psalm 72:1–2, 7–8, 12–13, 17
Gospel: Luke 10:21–24

READ

> For he rescues the poor when they cry out, the
> oppressed who have no one to help.
>
> —Psalm 72:12

REFLECT

For thousands of years, the Israelites waited for the coming of
the Messiah. Powerless to escape from slavery and oppression,
they longed for the day that the Savior would arrive to free them
from bondage.

Two thousand years after the birth of Jesus, we still find ourselves enslaved by sin, anxiety, and hopelessness. Focusing on
this harsh reality can easily lead to despair as we recognize just
how powerless we are. This verse from the psalm from today's
Mass reminds us that, even though we may be powerless, there
is someone capable of coming to our assistance. If we cry out
to the Lord, he will help us.

RESPOND

Ultimately, the fruitfulness of our Advent depends on God's
grace. That being the case, however, we still have a role to play.

We might not be able to take credit for our Advent successes, but we can take full credit for our failures. Despite God's willingness to help us and provide the grace we need to grow in holiness during this season, we have the power to thwart his efforts.

I wish it wasn't true, but we really do have the power to sabotage our Advent progress. Typically, this happens when we conclude that we're too far gone, we don't have enough time, or the effort required will be too great. Can you guess when this decision to give up usually takes place? If you guessed the beginning of Advent, you are correct. Therefore, *now* is the time to act to avoid giving up before you really get started.

What can we do to avoid giving up and losing the potential benefit of the Advent season? A careful reading of this verse gives us the answer: God rescues the poor and those who can't help themselves *when they cry out*. That's the key. The Lord will help us grow closer to him, but we must turn to him for help. Let's do it!

PRAY

Lord Jesus, as I continue to prepare for your arrival, it's easy to become overwhelmed by the amount of work that needs to be done. As I look back over my life, I see many wasted opportunities and spiritual failures. I'm tempted to just give up and say, "What's the point?" with the feeling that I don't have what it takes. This verse reminds me that you will always assist those who cry out to you for help. Sometimes, I try to fix everything on my own and become frustrated when I fail. Today, I recognize that I need your help, and I ask you to grant me the grace to be transformed this Advent. Thank you for the reminder that you will come to my assistance when I cry out to you. Amen.

Wednesday
FIRST WEEK OF ADVENT

Reading: Isaiah 25:6–10a
Responsorial Psalm: Psalm 23:1–3a, 3b–4, 5, 6
Gospel: Matthew 15:29–37

READ

> Jesus summoned his disciples and said, "My heart is
> moved with pity for the crowd, for they have been
> with me now for three days and have nothing to eat.
> I do not want to send them away hungry, for fear
> they may collapse on the way."
>
> —Matthew 15:32

REFLECT

Do you ever wonder why so many struggling individuals seek
comfort in television, sports, food, alcohol, or shopping instead
of turning to Jesus? It's probably because they don't know him
or he's not real enough to them. As this verse illustrates, however, not only is Jesus real, but he cares about our spiritual and
material needs.

There's believing in Jesus and then there's *believing* in Jesus.
The more we believe in the reality of Jesus, the more likely we
are to trust and follow him. In my *Give Up Worry for Lent* parish missions, I frequently make the point that Christians give
in to worry because Jesus is not real enough to them. I know
this challenge firsthand because I struggle with worry in my

own life. Sure, Jesus is real at Mass and when I read the Bible, but he often becomes "less real" when that unexpected illness, catastrophe, or repair bill arrives.

The problems of daily life often appear more real than the ever-present and all-loving Jesus Christ. That happens because we don't know him well enough. The more we rely on his love, power, and constant presence, the less likely we will panic when faced with a problem. Instead, we'll turn to him for help, knowing that he's bigger than any challenge we could ever face.

RESPOND

How real is Jesus to you? No matter how you answer, there's no need for alarm. One of the things we'll be working on throughout Advent is getting to know him better. And no matter how well you know him now, there's always room for improvement. Over the next few weeks, we'll hear him speak through the scriptures, we'll speak to him in prayer, and we'll encounter him in the sacraments. As a result, he will become more real to us, and our desire to follow him will increase.

Throughout Advent you'll hear a recurring theme about the need to make room for Jesus in your life. This involves eliminating the clutter that crowds him out. Focusing too much on the trials of life is a common trap and a great place to start this "cleaning." We'll do this not by ignoring our struggles, but by acknowledging that the Lord is bigger than the biggest problem we could ever face. The more we believe that truth, the more likely we'll be to turn away from panic and toward Jesus.

PRAY

Dear Jesus, as we head toward the celebration of your birth, I have to admit that I'm not always experiencing great joy. There are so many competing tasks and trials that are weighing me down. If I fully understood who you are, how much you love me, and just how in control you really are, I would feel much lighter. I desire that trust, Lord—I want you to become so real to me that I will face each day with total confidence in your care and provision. I'm looking forward to working on this trust in the days to come. Thank you for this season and for your willingness to help me. Amen.

Thursday
FIRST WEEK OF ADVENT

Reading Isaiah 26:1–6
Responsorial Psalm: Psalm 118:1, 8–9, 19–21, 25–27a
Gospel: Matthew 7:21, 24–27

READ

> Everyone who listens to these words of mine and acts on them will be like a wise man who built his house on rock. The rain fell, the floods came, and the winds blew and buffeted the house. But it did not collapse; it had been set solidly on rock.
>
> —Matthew 7:24–25

REFLECT

Do you ever panic when an unexpected crisis arises? As a "recovering" panicker (some days are better than others), I can personally vouch for the advice that Jesus is giving. If we listen to his words and put them into practice, we will be less likely to panic when things go wrong.

Over the next few weeks, we'll have the opportunity to listen to his messages on a daily basis. Some of the words will be spoken directly by Jesus, and others will be spoken or written by other biblical figures under the guidance of the Holy Spirit. The good news is that the Lord will be speaking to us in the pages of this book every day for the remainder of Advent. And as he promised, those who listen and act on his words will be able to live stormproof lives.

Before we move on, however, let's spend some time addressing the rain, floods, and wind mentioned by Jesus. Take note of the fact that he didn't say we *may* encounter storms in life. The word *if* doesn't appear anywhere in his weather forecast. Rather, he states that the rain *will* fall, the floods *will* come, the winds *will* blow, and our house *will* be buffeted. There's no getting around the fact that we will experience storms in life. If that's the case, why not take the Lord's advice so we'll be prepared?

RESPOND

As I mentioned, the Lord will be speaking to us daily for the remainder of Advent and we'll have many opportunities to listen to and act upon his words. Instead of waiting until tomorrow to begin, however, let's begin today by focusing on one of my favorite Bible verses. These words come straight from the mouth of Jesus and are directed to those of us who are weary: "Come to me, all you who labor and are burdened, and I will give you rest" (Mt 11:28).

In addition to what you're already facing, the next few weeks will provide the opportunity to become even more weary and burdened. Instead of losing sleep or worrying about that problem you're facing, take Jesus up on his offer and run into his arms. If you're not sure how to do it, try the words in the prayer below.

PRAY

Lord Jesus, I want to build my life on a solid foundation by listening to and acting on your words. Today, I'll choose to do just that and come to you in all my weariness. I could definitely use the rest you promised. Please help me to deal with the problems of daily living and grant me the peace that only you can give. Thank you. Amen.

Friday

FIRST WEEK OF ADVENT

Reading: Isaiah 29:17–24
Responsorial Psalm: Psalm 27:1, 4, 13–14
Gospel: Matthew 9:27–31

READ

> When he entered the house, the blind men approached him and Jesus said to them, "Do you believe that I can do this?" "Yes, Lord," they said to him.
>
> —Matthew 9:28

REFLECT

Before healing two blind men, Jesus asked them a simple question. He wanted to know if they believed in his power to heal them. Their two-word answer ("Yes, Lord") reveals the depth of their faith. They expressed their belief not only that Jesus is Lord but also that he had the power to cure their blindness.

Do you remember a few days ago when we discussed the importance of believing in Jesus? Today's verse continues that theme by posing a question we are called to answer multiple times every day. Just how much do we believe in the power and lordship of Jesus?

Prior to this verse, Matthew writes that the two blind men followed Jesus, crying out, "Son of David, have pity on us!" This one sentence reveals the depth of their belief in Jesus. By using the messianic title *Son of David*, they are acknowledging Jesus as Lord and Savior, and their request to "have pity on us" illustrates their belief that he can help them. And although Jesus undoubtedly already knows the answer, he gives the men an opportunity to affirm their faith by asking if they believe he can heal them. He immediately responds by saying, "Let it be done for you *according to your faith*" (emphasis mine). Once again, according to Jesus, faith really does matter.

RESPOND

What do you need Jesus to do for you today? It may be something you're already praying for, or it may be something so impossible that you haven't even considered bringing it to Jesus. As you think of that need, imagine Jesus asking you the same question he asked the blind men: "Do you believe that I can do this?" How would you respond?

If we dig deep enough, most of us can come up with some intention that seems hopeless. It could be an end to world hunger, a greater respect for the sanctity of life, the healing of an illness, or the return of a loved one to the Church. Don't panic over your feeling of hopelessness. Faith is more than a feeling. We don't know how the blind men felt inside. After all, faith always involves some degree of uncertainty. What we do know is that they chose to believe in the power of Jesus and accept him as their Lord and Savior. You can choose to do the same thing by presenting your "hopeless" situation to him today. Give Jesus a chance to perform a miracle in your life. Don't stop there, however. While you're at it, ask Jesus to increase your confidence in him so much that the word *hopeless* isn't in your vocabulary.

PRAY

Dear Jesus, even though I want to believe, I have to admit that sometimes I lack confidence in your power. If I was blind, I'm not so sure I would confidently believe you could heal me miraculously. But here's the thing, Lord: I know my faith is lacking, but I believe you can help me. Please increase my faith so I can approach you with the certainty of the two blind men. Thank you, Lord. Amen.

Saturday
FIRST WEEK OF ADVENT

Reading: Isaiah 30:19–21, 23–26
Responsorial Psalm: Psalm 147:1–2, 3–4, 5–6
Gospel: Matthew 9:35–10:1, 5a, 6–8

READ

> At the sight of the crowds, his heart was moved
> with pity for them because they were troubled and
> abandoned, like sheep without a shepherd.
> —Matthew 9:36

REFLECT

When Jesus saw the crowds who were very much in need of
spiritual guidance, he was moved with pity and took action.
Summoning his disciples, he gave them the necessary authority
to minister in his name and sent them out to the people. While
this is very good news, what moves me the most is the human
heart of Jesus the Good Shepherd feeling sad for the abandoned
sheep.

Sometimes we focus so much on the divinity of Jesus that
we lose sight of the fact that he has human emotions. Like us,
he can feel happy, sad, or lonely. In this case, he sees that the
crowds are troubled and abandoned and actually feels sorrowful
because of it. Before moving on to how he responded, let's linger
on how he felt. Jesus was sad.

As the first week of Advent draws to a close, there's a good chance you're feeling lost, overwhelmed, or just plain sad. Maybe you're feeling discouraged because of a lack of spiritual progress, or maybe you're just not feeling the joy of the Christmas season. Take comfort in the fact that Jesus understands your situation and feels your pain.

RESPOND

As you go through the day today, remember that Jesus can see you. He's aware of your struggles. It makes him sad when you feel hopeless or overwhelmed. No matter how lonely or abandoned you feel, you are never alone. If you're suffering in any way, Jesus is with you and shares in your suffering. In addition to being sad, Jesus can also experience the emotion of happiness. Whenever you're happy, Jesus shares in your happiness.

Finally, as comforting as it is to focus on the human emotions of Jesus, we don't want to forget about his divine power. As indicated in the "sheep without a shepherd" description, his sadness over the crowd's helplessness is followed by his direct intervention in the situation. That's what is referred to as divine mercy. Jesus is never content to simply stand by, feeling sorry for you as you suffer. He wants to do more, but not at the expense of your free will. He remains by your side waiting for you to invite him into your life. Doing so will give you the comforting divine assistance you need. It will also make Jesus very happy.

PRAY

Dear Jesus, sometimes I forget that you have the ability to be sad. As I look at your reaction to the abandoned crowd, however, it becomes clear that you can and do experience human emotions. It's even more mind-boggling to picture you getting sad over my personal struggles, Jesus. With all of the suffering going on in the world, how is it that you care about me on such an intimate level? Nevertheless, I know that you do. Speaking of emotions, I want to do what I can to contribute to your happiness. By trying to draw closer to you during Advent, I know that's what will happen. Please grant me the grace to make this a fruitful Advent. Not only will that make me happy, but I know it will make you happy too. Thank you, Lord. Amen.

SECOND WEEK OF ADVENT

It's Happening Now!

Second Sunday of Advent
YEAR A

First Reading: Isaiah 11:1–10
Responsorial Psalm: Psalm 72:1–2, 7–8, 12–13, 17
Second Reading: Romans 15:4–9
Gospel: Matthew 3:1–12

READ

John the Baptist appeared, preaching in the desert of Judea and saying, "Repent, for the kingdom of heaven is at hand!" It was of him that the prophet Isaiah had spoken when he said: "A voice of one crying out in the desert, Prepare the way of the Lord, make straight his paths."

—Matthew 3:1–3

REFLECT

As we enter the second week of Advent, we're greeted with an urgent call to action and an Old Testament reference from John the Baptist. John informs his listeners that the prophecy of the Messiah's arrival has come true. He follows it up with a call to repentance. Changes need to be made in order to enter the kingdom.

Unlike us, the people to whom John spoke were waiting for the initial arrival of the Messiah, hence the reference to Isaiah's prophetic message. Like us, however, the people needed to do some spiritual housecleaning in order to properly welcome Jesus into their lives. What kind of housecleaning is needed?

In the original Greek manuscript of Matthew's gospel, the word translated as "repent" implies an internal change of heart or conversion. Like the people who first heard John's proclamation, we are being called to change the way we think and believe. This internal conversion is a daily exercise that needs to begin now. For them and for us, this is a great way to prepare to encounter Jesus in the Christmas feast.

RESPOND

Before we can make internal changes, as recommended by John the Baptist, we need to identify our problem areas. While this will be an ongoing process throughout our Advent journey, it would be a good idea to identify one or two areas for improvement now, before we go too much further.

What are some possible problem areas? Maybe you don't know Jesus as well as you'd like, struggle with impatience or anger, rarely pray or read the Bible, don't attend Mass regularly, or haven't been to Confession in a long time. Don't panic if nothing immediately comes to mind. Sometimes the conversion process is more of a fine-tuning operation than a massive spiritual overhaul. Whatever the case, let's start with a simple exercise.

Jesus's own example gives us the perfect model for how we should think, speak, and act. We all fall short to some degree, so a conversion or internal change is needed. Because of our fallen human nature, however, we can't make the necessary changes on our own. The Holy Spirit was sent to assist and lead us. How should a Spirit-led life look? According to St. Paul (see Galatians 5:22–23), the fruits of the Holy Spirit are love, joy, peace, patience, kindness, goodness, faithfulness, gentleness, and self-control. These supernatural virtues were very apparent in the life of Jesus but are not always so apparent in our lives. Reading slowly and prayerfully through the list of fruits should give you an idea of where your conversion should begin.

PRAY

Dear Jesus, as I read through the fruits of the Holy Spirit, I recognize that I need to make some changes. I desire for my life to look more like yours, but I can't do it on my own. Please awaken your Holy Spirit in me to help me identify my problem areas and assist me in making the changes needed. I look forward to growing closer to you throughout Advent and producing the good fruit that you desire. Amen.

Second Sunday of Advent
YEAR B

First Reading: Isaiah 40:1–5, 9–11
Responsorial Psalm: Psalm 85:9–10, 11–12, 13–14
Second Reading: 2 Peter 3:8–14
Gospel: Mark 1:1–8

READ

> One mightier than I is coming after me. I am not worthy to stoop and loosen the thongs of his sandals. I have baptized you with water; he will baptize you with the holy Spirit.
>
> —Mark 1:7–8

REFLECT

The Gospel from today's Mass begins with an Old Testament reference to the prophet Isaiah, as he writes about a messenger sent to "prepare the way of the Lord." Rather abruptly, Mark shifts to the appearance of John the Baptist in the desert, who calls for a baptism of repentance for the forgiveness of sins. It becomes rather obvious that John is the prophesied messenger sent to prepare for the coming of the Messiah.

We're told that all the inhabitants of Jerusalem were being baptized by John in the Jordan River as they acknowledged their sins. After a very brief description of the garb and dietary habits of John, Mark's gospel records his proclamation of the coming of the Mighty One who will baptize with the Holy Spirit. Of course, he's referring to Jesus Christ—the long-awaited Messiah.

John's message is one we all need to hear as we enter the second week of Advent. The Messiah is coming, and we need to prepare for his arrival. How do we do it? The best way to get ready to welcome Jesus is by making room in our lives for him.

RESPOND

If the idea of setting aside time that you don't have during the busiest time of the year sounds overwhelming to you, here's some good news: you're already doing it! By spending a few minutes to read this reflection, you've made the conscious decision to take a break from the world's craziness in order to prepare for Jesus's arrival in your life.

As we listen to the words of John the Baptist, we're reminded of the power contained in the Sacrament of Baptism. When we're baptized, we receive the Holy Spirit and the power that comes with his presence. Not feeling the power? Don't panic. We'll be working on this for the next few weeks.

Our ultimate goal in welcoming Jesus is to allow him to work in and through us. Others should be able to see Jesus in our words and actions. This transformation occurs through the work of the Holy Spirit. In baptism, we receive what we need to be other-Christs to the world. We simply have to tap into the power we already have. Let's not get ahead of ourselves, however. Today's goal is to anticipate and desire what our lives will look like when the power of the Spirit is awakened in us.

PRAY

Dear Jesus, as I listen to the words of John the Baptist, I'm reminded of the power that came to me when I was baptized. I may not be able to feel the power, but I now know I have it. As we head into the second week of Advent, I ask you to awaken your Holy Spirit in me. Please guide my thoughts, words, and actions so that I resemble you more each day. I believe you have the power to do this, Lord. Although I am weak, I find my strength in you. Amen.

Second Sunday of Advent
YEAR C

First Reading: Baruch 5:1–9
Responsorial Psalm: Psalm 126:1–2, 2–3, 4–5, 6
Second Reading: Philippians 1:4–6, 8–11
Gospel: Luke 3:1–6

READ

> The word of God came to John the son of Zechariah in the desert. He went throughout [the] whole region of the Jordan, proclaiming a baptism of repentance for the forgiveness of sins.
>
> —Luke 3:2–3

REFLECT

Today's gospel begins in "the fifteenth year of the reign of Tiberius Caesar" when Pontius Pilate was governor of Judea and Herod was tetrarch of Galilee. Luke then continues his account with a series of unusual names and places such as Lysanias, Annas, Caiphas, Ituraea, and Trachonitis. Luke is going to great lengths to place John the Baptist at a particular point in history, so it's critical for us to understand where he was and what happened while he was there.

Luke informs us that "the word of God came to John . . . in the desert." Although that encounter remains somewhat mysterious, we do know that it took place, and that it took place in the desert, a quiet place devoid of the distractions of the world.

After encountering the word of God, he went out proclaiming his message of repentance and preparation. We don't need to know the details of the conversation to know that John had a profound encounter with God's word that launched his prophetic ministry.

The isolation of the desert was a great place to hear the Lord's voice. Free from the commotion of the world, John was able to receive the instructions that he would deliver to a waiting world. Since the salvation of humanity was riding on his words, it's a good thing he was able to clearly hear his instructions.

RESPOND

The world can be a very noisy place. As a result, it can be very difficult to hear God's voice. Even good "noise" such as Christmas music, shopping, and celebrations can drown out the Lord's message. In order to hear him speak and to prepare to welcome him more deeply, we need to imitate John and find our way into our own deserts.

If the thought of retreating into a deserted area during the craziness of the Advent season seems overwhelming, I have good news for you. As you read this, you're already in your "desert." While communicating with God is best done in a secluded area, it's not necessary to leave your house. The most important thing for you to do is seek that internal quiet disposition that allows you to encounter the Lord. By reading and reflecting on the Bible verse for today, you allowed the Lord to speak to you. And by praying the words below, you are speaking to him.

Each of the reflections in this book provides you with daily "desert" time needed to encounter the Lord. In doing so, you'll be prepared to welcome him more deeply into your life in our

Christmas feast. And like John the Baptist, you'll then be able to bring the Good News into the world as you share the peace that comes from a relationship with Jesus Christ.

PRAY

Dear Jesus, thank you for allowing me to spend this time with you. Even though these reflections take only a few minutes, I know these daily exercises will help me maintain my peace throughout the day. Any time spent with you is always time well spent. As I move forward, Lord, help me to remain faithful to these daily devotions and spend time in the "desert" with you. In the weeks to come, I know I'm going to feel increased pressure to give up. With your assistance, however, I know this can be a fruitful Advent. Please grant me the grace I need to make it happen. Amen.

Monday

SECOND WEEK OF ADVENT

Reading: Isaiah 35:1–10
Responsorial Psalm: Psalm 85:9ab, 10, 11–12, 13–14
Gospel: Luke 5:17–26

READ

> Be strong, do not fear! Here is your God, he comes
> with vindication; With divine recompense he comes
> to save you.
>
> —Isaiah 35:4

REFLECT

Taken from the first reading of today's Mass, these words from
the prophet Isaiah are meant to give comfort and strength to
those who are afraid. Throughout the Old and New Testaments,
the "be not afraid" message appears hundreds of times. Why
should God's people have no fear? It's because of not the absence
of danger but rather the presence of God.

When Isaiah first proclaimed these words, the people were
awaiting the arrival of the Messiah. They knew he would come
to save them in some way. They may not have understood how
the saving would take place or when it would happen, but they
believed it would happen. The words of Isaiah were designed to
strengthen their belief and give them hope. There's no reason to
be afraid. The Messiah is on his way. Everything will work out.

In a similar way, we can look to Jesus to deliver us from our fear. As we prepare to welcome him more fully into our lives, we tap into feeling the hopeful expectation experienced by the Israelites thousands of years ago. When the Lord arrives, things will get better. Even though the world may still be a frightening place, we don't have to be afraid because Jesus is with us.

RESPOND

Just as often happens during Lent, our Advent exercises focus mainly on repentance and conversion. While that is a big part of the preparation process, we should also keep our eyes on the prize. A life centered on Jesus is going to be a whole lot less stressful. The more we welcome him into our lives, the more peace we'll experience.

Although Jesus was born primarily to liberate us from our sins, he also came to free us from excess fear and worry. Therefore, as you continue your Advent preparation to welcome him more fully into your life, you can also look forward to the greater peace he will bring.

As we read the words of Isaiah today, let's anticipate the joy that is headed our way. Yes, there is work involved, but we're already in our second week of preparing. The Lord is on his way to us, and we're making room. Along with his arrival comes the promise of greater peace and a decrease in fear.

PRAY

Lord Jesus, Prince of Peace, sometimes life seems like one burden after another. With so many things to worry about, I often feel overwhelmed. As I continue to prepare to welcome you more deeply into my life, I look forward to the increased peace you will bring. Please continue to fill me with hope and grant me the grace to continue moving closer to you. Amen.

Tuesday

SECOND WEEK OF ADVENT

Reading: Isaiah 40:1–11
Responsorial Psalm: Psalm 96:1–2, 3, 10ac, 11–12, 13
Gospel: Matthew 18:12–14

READ

> If a man has a hundred sheep and one of them goes
> astray, will he not leave the ninety-nine in the hills
> and go in search of the stray?
>
> —Matthew 18:12

REFLECT

To express how much the heavenly Father loves his children,
Jesus uses the short parable of the lost sheep. In this brief narrative, the Lord invites his listeners to consider a man who possesses one hundred sheep. When one of them wanders off, he
leaves the ninety-nine to search for the one who is lost. That
one sheep is so important to him that he won't rest until it is
brought safely home.

Like the sheep that wanders off, we often don't even realize
we're lost. Because of that blindness, it's difficult to get back on
track unless someone intervenes. That's why Jesus came into
our world. His mission was to seek out the lost sheep and draw
them back to the Father.

We often feel we're the ones seeking to draw closer to Jesus,
especially during the Advent season. While it's true that we have

to seek him in order to find him, this verse reminds us of an important fact: Jesus has been searching for you long before you began searching for him. As much as you desire to grow closer to him during Advent, he desires it even more. You really matter to him. Pretty amazing, isn't it?

RESPOND

As we continue our Advent preparations, here's something to consider. The Lord wants us to succeed even more than we do. And because he is divine and can provide unlimited help to us in the form of grace, the odds of succeeding are definitely in our favor.

That said, it's still highly unlikely that any of us will be perfect in our Advent preparations. There will be days when we are distracted and mentally or physically absent. It happens. Sometimes life and its distractions get the best of us. If and when this happens, we can take comfort in the fact that someone will seek us out and help get us back on track.

I highly recommend that you make a sincere effort to keep up with these daily reflections, but don't give up if something happens and you miss one here or there. The parable of the lost sheep reminds us that the Good Shepherd will not rest until we're back where we belong. If we wander off and lose our Advent focus, he'll come looking for us and meet us where we are. Together, we'll get back to where we need to be.

PRAY

Dear Jesus, sometimes I forget how much you love me. Thank you for constantly searching for me, especially when I stray.

My desire for the remainder of Advent is to draw closer to you each day. I will try to do my best, but it's good to know that you won't give up on me if I mess up. Please help me to keep going, one day at a time. Thank you, Lord. Amen.

Wednesday
SECOND WEEK OF ADVENT

Reading: Isaiah 40:25–31
Responsorial Psalm: Psalm 103:1–2, 3–4, 8, 10
Gospel: Matthew 11:28–30

READ

> Come to me, all you who labor and are burdened,
> and I will give you rest.
>
> —Matthew 11:28

REFLECT

If you're looking for peace, this Bible verse tells you all you need to know. With these familiar words, Jesus invites all who are weary and burdened to come to him and receive the rest they seek. There are no qualifications or fine print, just an unqualified offer. If we come to him, we will receive peace.

While it's true that coming to Jesus will bring peace, it's important to understand that it's not a one-time event. Rather, it's a gradual one-day-at-a-time series of steps that draw us closer to him. As we draw closer and closer to him, we will experience more peace. As you may have already figured out, that's exactly what we're doing in this series of Advent reflections. By reading and reflecting on his words, day by day we are gradually drawing closer to Jesus.

Listening to the words of Jesus is only part of the process, however. It's also expected that we respond in some way. We'll discuss it more in the section below, but this response typically involves our willingness to follow Jesus wherever he leads. Even though this will involve daily crosses and suffering, the promise of peace remains. If we strive to seek Jesus in our daily circumstances, we will receive the peace that only he can give. It's a peace that cannot be taken away by earthly trials.

RESPOND

It's easy to become burdened and weary, especially during this time of year. Today, Jesus offers to give us the rest we seek. All he asks is that we come to him. As you read this and reflect on his words, you're doing just that. Right now, nothing else matters. This is your "Jesus time." While you're spending this time with him, millions of other people are frantically rushing around getting ready for Christmas. You, on the other hand, are focusing on Jesus. Even though it takes only a few minutes, this is definitely time well spent.

Depending on when you're reading this, the rest of this day or the next will be filled with people, events, and circumstances. Why not invite Jesus to face the day with you and share your experiences with him? Spending time alone with him is important, but there's no reason your prayer time can't spill out into your active life. The ultimate goal of our Advent preparation is to invite Jesus more deeply into your daily circumstances. Not only is that what he wants, but also it's what will give you the peace you seek.

PRAY

Dear Jesus, what a perfect time to hear your words. I'm feeling especially burdened today and could use some rest. You said if I would come to you, you would give me rest. Here I am. It's great to spend some time with you. As refreshing as this is, however, I'd like to invite you to share my life with me. I'd like to bring you with me everywhere I go. In doing so, I'll never be alone—that sounds really good to me. Thank you, Lord. Amen.

Thursday
SECOND WEEK OF ADVENT

Reading: Isaiah 41:13–20
Responsorial Psalm: Psalm 145:1, 9, 10–11, 12–13ab
Gospel: Matthew 11:11–15

READ

> For I am the LORD, your God, who grasp your right
> hand; It is I who say to you, Do not fear, I will help
> you.
>
> —Isaiah 41:13

REFLECT

We may not always be able to understand God's actions, but
we can be sure that he has his reasons. The same can be true
for his words. As can be seen in the first thirty-seven chapters
of the Book of Job, the Lord speaks only when necessary. Even
though Job asked God many questions, it took a long time to
get a response. And when God spoke, he spoke in a *big* way.

Unlike many of us, God doesn't speak needlessly. When
he speaks, it's because someone needs to hear what he has to
say. These words, directed to Elijah, are no exception. The Lord
is telling the prophet something that needed to be heard. The
Israelites needed to hear that they were not alone, that the Lord
was close enough to grasp their right hand, and that he would
help them. Why was it necessary for Isaiah to deliver this message to God's people? They needed to hear these words because

they felt abandoned, helpless, and afraid. They had no idea that the all-loving, all-powerful God was in their midst, ready and willing to assist them.

When the Lord first delivered these words to his people, they were awaiting the coming of the Messiah. Even though God was present to them, the birth of Jesus is the ultimate fulfillment of the prophecy. After all, the Lord can't get much closer than taking on a human body and literally entering into the world! As we prepare to celebrate the birth of Jesus, let's look at this verse through the eyes of the fearful and lonely people eagerly awaiting the Lord's arrival into their world. In a sense, that's exactly who we are too. The good news is that he's on his way.

RESPOND

While this message should be great news for anyone who feels lonely, afraid, and powerless, it can sometimes be interpreted as theoretical fluff. For many years that's exactly how I responded when I heard these words. Even though I believed Jesus came into our world, died for my sins, and rose from the dead, I lived my life as though he didn't exist. I didn't live a totally immoral life, but I lived an empty and often hopeless life. The problems and challenges I faced every day were real to me, but Jesus wasn't. I had no clue that he was close enough to hold my hand and could literally help me with my problems. Then one day things began to change. The Holy Spirit opened my heart and made me aware that I wasn't alone.

Even if you're not feeling totally hopeless and alone, we can all use a greater sense of the Lord's presence. Because our relationship with him is based on faith, we grow closer to him gradually. It's something we'll be working on for the rest of our lives. Right now, however, let's set our sights on Christmas. The one who grasps our right hand and tells us to have no fear is on his way. Hold out your right hand and look at it. It may look empty now, but not for long. Jesus will help us as much as we let him. Let's get excited and do what we can to make room for him.

PRAY

Dear Jesus, it's so refreshing to imagine you holding my right hand and helping me with my problems. I desperately need you in my life, but I struggle to feel your presence. I'm willing to do what I can to grow closer to you, and that's why I'm reading this book and praying this prayer. I can't do it without your help, Lord. Please help me. I look forward to the day when I can confidently believe the words you spoke to Isaiah. I know that day is approaching. Thank you, Jesus. Amen.

Friday

SECOND WEEK OF ADVENT

Reading: Isaiah 48:17–19
Responsorial Psalm: Psalm 1:1–2, 3, 4, 6
Gospel: Matthew 11:16–19

READ

> Thus says the LORD, your redeemer, the Holy One of
> Israel: I, the LORD, your God, teach you what is for
> your good, and lead you on the way you should go.
> —Isaiah 48:17

REFLECT

Before the birth of Jesus, people often viewed God as a distant
and frightening ruler. Things began to change, however, when
the long-awaited Messiah entered the world as a vulnerable
infant. Throughout his public ministry, Jesus not only taught
us about God but also gave us the ultimate example of how to
live our lives. As we listen to his words, observe his actions, and
explore the teachings of the Church, we allow him to teach us
the meaning of life and how we should live each day.

As we prepare to celebrate the birth of Jesus, we'll not only
look at what the prophets and others said about him but also
listen to his words and observe his actions. In addition, we'll
examine the Lord's guidance as he speaks through his Church.

The best way to welcome him is to learn who he is, why he matters, and how he fits into our lives.

But why should we stop there? Since Isaiah reminds us of the Lord's desire to teach us what is for our good and lead us in the way we should go, let's ask him to guide us in our Advent preparation. Jesus knows our problem areas better than we do. It's hard to imagine it, but he also desires a close relationship with us even more than we do. It only makes sense to involve him in the process. Let's do it!

RESPOND

What is blocking you from growing closer to Jesus? What do you have to do less or more of in order to let him work more fully in your life? Many times we just don't know. When we look at the words of the prophet Isaiah, however, we're reminded of something that's easily overlooked: God will lead us. If we're unsure of how to proceed during Advent, let's ask the Holy Spirit to help us.

The Bible verses, reflections, and exercises in this book are basically guidelines. Even though they're somewhat specific, we're all going to come away with slightly different takeaways. What I consider a key point may be relatively minor to you and vice versa. When we read or reflect on a Bible verse, the Holy Spirit will often lead us to completely different courses of action. That's a good thing. He really does know what we need and how we should proceed. In the following prayer, let's act on the Lord's promise as spoken through the words of Isaiah. Instead of trying to take control of our Advent preparation, let's turn it over to the Lord. He'll lead and we'll follow. What could be better?

PRAY

Dear Jesus, as I continue to walk through Advent with you, I'm going to take the advice you gave through the prophet Isaiah. Please teach me what is for my good and lead me in the way I should go. Starting today, guide my thoughts as I read and reflect on your inspired words in the Bible. Awaken your Holy Spirit in so that I can be led along the path that will best help me to prepare to receive you. I believe your promise as recorded in the Bible, and I ask you to lead me throughout the remainder of Advent. Thank you and Amen.

Saturday

SECOND WEEK OF ADVENT

Reading: Sirach 48:1–4, 9–11
Responsorial Psalm: Psalm 80:2ac, 3b, 15–16, 18–19
Gospel: Luke 17:9a, 10–13

READ

> Then the disciples understood that he was speaking to them of John the Baptist.
>
> —Matthew 17:13

REFLECT

In the Gospel from today's Mass, we get to eavesdrop on a conversation between Jesus and his disciples as they are coming down from the mountain. Having just witnessed the Lord's transfiguration and seeing him in his glorified form, they were probably still dazed. They asked him about the scribes' belief that Elijah would return immediately before the coming of the Messiah, referencing this passage: "Now I am sending to you Elijah the prophet. Before the day of the LORD comes, the great and terrible day; He will turn the heart of fathers to their sons, and the heart of sons to their fathers, Lest I come and strike the land with utter destruction" (Mal 3:23–24).

When Jesus stated that "Elijah has already come," they understood that he was speaking of John the Baptist. The scribes were correct in their understanding that "Elijah" would precede the Messiah's arrival but missed the point that John the Baptist was serving as this modern-day "Elijah." Because of the short-sightedness, they failed to take John seriously and ignored his call to repentance.

At the beginning of this second week of Advent, we read about John the Baptist as he urged the people to get ready for Jesus. He called them to an interior conversion of heart and a corresponding change in their actions. To paraphrase his message: The Messiah is here, and the kingdom of God is now present on earth. There's still time to get ready, but you must do it now!

Those who recognized John's role as the new "Elijah" paid attention, while those who didn't ignored him. Jesus cleared up the confusion for his disciples, and they recognized the legitimacy of John the Baptist and his message. As the second week of Advent comes to a close, we would be wise to do the same.

RESPOND

Before entering the third week of Advent, it would be a good idea to go back and revisit this past Sunday's reflection. The endorsement he received from Jesus makes it even more important to listen to John and follow his advice.

As you read these words, our celebration of the arrival of Jesus on Christmas Day is drawing near. With each passing day, we get closer to the big day. John urges us to prepare—and that's exactly what we're doing. It's normal to feel a sense of urgency, but there's no need to panic. With the help of the Spirit, our spiritual housecleaning operation is moving forward, and we're heading in the right direction.

Tomorrow, we'll enter the third week of Advent, and we'll experience a slight shift in tone. The focus during the first week was on watching; the second week was centered on action. As we enter into the third week, the emphasis will be on rejoicing. Why do we rejoice? We rejoice because the Lord is coming soon—*very* soon!

PRAY

Dear Jesus, I can understand why the scribes misunderstood the role of Elijah. Thank you for explaining that the scriptures actually referred to John the Baptist. Understanding his role helps me to pay even greater attention to his words. I'll make a point to read his instructions again and follow them attentively. Thank you for helping me prepare to receive you. Even though the clock is ticking, I realize there's no need to panic. I'll continue to do my best and depend on you for the rest. I'm excited to enter into the next week because I know we are nearing our celebration of your arrival. Thank you, Jesus. Amen.

THIRD WEEK OF ADVENT

Rejoice!

Third Sunday of Advent
YEAR A

First Reading: Isaiah 35:1–6a, 10
Responsorial Psalm: Psalm 146:6–7, 8–9, 9–10
Second Reading: James 5:7–10
Gospel: Matthew 11:2–11

READ

> Be patient, therefore, brothers, until the coming of the Lord. See how the farmer waits for the precious fruit of the earth, being patient with it until it receives the early and the late rains. You too must be patient. Make your hearts firm, because the coming of the Lord is at hand.
>
> —James 5:7–8

REFLECT

It's easy to lose patience, especially when the fruits of one's labor can't be seen. In this passage, James encourages us to remain patient until the coming of the Lord. Pointing to a farmer waiting for the fruit of the earth, he commands us (as evidenced by the use of the word *must*) to be patient and make our hearts firm because the coming of the Lord is at hand.

No doubt about it, waiting can be a big motivation killer—especially when no progress can be seen. Over time, it's easy to give in to a "what's the use" mentality. In some cases, this isn't a big deal, but in the case of waiting for the Lord, it can be disastrous. The phrases "must be patient" and "make your hearts firm" are designed to capture the attention of those who may be losing patience and create in them a sense of urgency.

It's important to note why a farmer continues to wait even when the fruits of his planting can't be seen. The farmer waits because he knows that what he has planted will eventually produce fruit. Ultimately, it comes down to a matter of faith. Similarly, it's by faith that we believe the Lord will come again and that our Advent exercises will produce good fruit.

RESPOND

These words, taken from today's second reading, are perfect for this season of waiting. Even more perfect, however, is that the Church chose to focus on the virtue of patience at this point in the Advent season. Having completed two weeks of preparation, the temptation to give up becomes increasingly real. It could be because we haven't seen enough spiritual progress, or it could just be that we're getting tired, but it should come as no surprise if you're feeling this today.

Because of this, it's providential that the Church emphasizes the "rejoice" theme on this Third Sunday of Advent. In keeping with this theme, the priest or deacon wears rose-colored vestments on this day. This external symbol reminds us that "the coming of the Lord is at hand." We may be tired or frustrated, but there is good reason to "make our hearts firm" and persevere. The finish line is closer than ever. We rejoice and keep moving forward not necessarily because we see but because we believe.

PRAY

I'm starting to get excited, Jesus. Even though I may not see or feel the fruit of my Advent labor, I choose to believe that it will happen. I know that you desire to draw closer to me and become more active in my life, and that's what keeps me going. In a few weeks, I believe you and I will be closer than ever before. For that reason, I join with the Church in rejoicing. Amen.

NOTE: The last eight days before Christmas comprise a special last phase of Advent preparation. This book addresses that period in a special section, so when the calendar turns to December 17, jump ahead to "Weekdays of Advent: December 17–24" on page 99 to resume your daily reflections.

Third Sunday of Advent
YEAR B

First Reading: Isaiah 61:1–2a, 10–11
Responsorial Psalm: Luke 1:46–48, 49–50, 53–54
Second Reading: 1 Thessalonians 5:16–24
Gospel: John 1:6–8, 19–28

READ

> May the God of peace himself make you perfectly holy and may you entirely, spirit, soul, and body, be preserved blameless for the coming of our Lord Jesus Christ. The one who calls you is faithful, and he will also accomplish it.
>
> —1 Thessalonians 5:23–24

REFLECT

Whether you're preparing for the Second Coming of Jesus or preparing to welcome him more deeply into your life at Christmas, these words offer encouragement and hope. As we continue to do what we can to prepare for Jesus, Paul removes some of the pressure by reminding us that becoming holy is not something we do on our own. Ultimately, the Lord is the only one who can increase our holiness. He certainly expects us to do our part to prepare for the arrival of Jesus, but our spiritual growth depends on his grace.

Did you notice that Paul refers to God as the "God of peace"? By using this phrase, he reminds us why we may have opened this book in the first place: peace. This supernatural gift is produced organically whenever we make an effort to follow the Lord. Because it does not depend on external circumstances, we can find it in the middle of a storm or in the craziness of the pre-Christmas madness. Even when our main goal is preparing for Jesus, peace is a natural byproduct of that process.

The final point to consider is God's role in our desire to become holy. Not only is he the one responsible for our success, but also he's responsible for planting the seed in the first place. As Paul reminds us in this passage, any desire to prepare for the coming of Christ comes from God. Most of the time we don't realize it, but he is the one calling us! And because he is faithful, we can count on him to finish what he started.

RESPOND

Today is the Third Sunday of Advent, and recognizing that we could be getting burned out or frustrated, the Church wisely includes an important reminder in the second reading to lift our hearts toward joyful anticipation. Throughout the Mass readings and responses, the word "rejoice" is used repeatedly, and the priest and deacon wear rose-colored vestments. This is done to remind us that Jesus is getting closer and to encourage us to persevere in our preparation.

As the season of Advent progresses and our Christmas "to do" list grows longer, we may feel the desire to put our spiritual exercises on the back burner. The desire to give up can intensify when we look back over the past two weeks and fail to see significant progress. When that happens, it's time to look closely at this Bible passage and recall that God—not us—is the one in charge of our Advent efforts. And since he doesn't quit and likes to complete what he begins, we're in great shape. As long as we don't give up, we will make progress and grow in holiness during Advent. For that reason, it is entirely appropriate to rejoice!

PRAY

Dear Jesus, you must have read my mind. As we begin the third week of Advent, I'm starting to feel a little burned out. It doesn't seem as if I'm making the progress I should make. As the date of our celebration of your arrival draws near, I don't feel I'm getting anywhere. Inspired by the message from St. Paul, however, I'm going to put aside my feelings and choose to keep moving forward. Please grant me the grace I need to continue to prepare to celebrate your presence with us. I rejoice as I look forward to your increased presence in my life. Amen.

NOTE: The last eight days before Christmas comprise a special last phase of Advent preparation. This book addresses that period in a special section, so when the calendar turns to December 17, jump ahead to "Weekdays of Advent: December 17–24" on page 99 to resume your daily reflections.

Third Sunday of Advent
YEAR C

First Reading: Zephaniah 3:14–18a
Responsorial Psalm: Isaiah 12:2–3, 4, 5–6
Second Reading: Philippians 4:4–7
Gospel: Luke 3:10–18

READ

> The LORD, your God, is in your midst, a mighty savior, Who will rejoice over you with gladness, and renew you in his love, Who will sing joyfully because of you, as on festival days.
>
> —Zephaniah 3:17–18a

REFLECT

Rejoice! Throughout the pages of the Bible, we are encouraged to rejoice. While it's commonly viewed as a reaction to favorable circumstances, the act of rejoicing is much more than that. As Christians, we are commanded to rejoice because our all-loving, all-powerful God is with us. Never is this more apparent than during the Advent season when we wait for the arrival of the one whose name (Emmanuel) literally means "God with us." Therefore, when we consider the closeness of our God, how could we not rejoice?

What's unusual about this Bible passage, however, is who does the rejoicing. While Zephaniah does call attention to the fact that our God and savior is in our midst, he doesn't command us to rejoice. Amazingly, he points out that *God himself* is rejoicing because we are in his midst. And not only does the Lord rejoice over us, but also he sings joyfully "as on festival days." He does this not because of what we do but because we are in his presence.

When I think about the Lord rejoicing and singing just because I'm with him, I don't need Zephaniah or anyone else to encourage me to rejoice. Merely thinking about the idea causes me to overflow with joy!

RESPOND

While joy is certainly an underlying theme of Advent, we *really* focus on it today. In fact, the Third Sunday of Advent is traditionally referred to as Gaudete Sunday from the Latin word for "rejoice." Because of this, I can't think of a better message than the one proclaimed by Zephaniah in today's first reading.

For many of us, the idea that God would rejoice just because we're with him is mind-boggling. As the prophet Zephaniah makes clear, however, it's absolutely true. The mere thought of being with us makes Almighty God rejoice. And because of his love for us, he wasn't content to simply rejoice from a distance. Instead, he devised a way to get as close to us as possible, choosing to take on human flesh and literally enter our world as a baby.

As you reflect on that today, don't just follow your feelings. Make the conscious decision to rejoice over the fact that Almighty God is rejoicing because he gets to share your life with you. That's why we wait joyfully and expectantly for the event that we will celebrate in a few short weeks. He's on his way to us, even now. Rejoice!

PRAY

Dear Jesus, sometimes it's difficult to comprehend how much you love me. Even among my close friends and loved ones I sometimes feel I have to earn their love. Therefore, I struggle with the idea that someone as important as you could love me unconditionally just for who I am. Even though I may not feel it, however, I do believe it. Thank you for rejoicing over me. I'll continue to do what I can to prepare for your arrival. Today's preparation will involve rejoicing over the anticipation that soon we will be celebrating your coming among us to share our lives. I can't wait, Lord! Amen.

NOTE: The last eight days before Christmas comprise a special last phase of Advent preparation. This book addresses that period in a special section, so when the calendar turns to December 17, jump ahead to "Weekdays of Advent: December 17–24" on page 99 to resume your daily reflections.

Monday

THIRD WEEK OF ADVENT

Reading: Numbers 24:2–7, 15–17a
Responsorial Psalm: Psalm 25:4–5ab, 6, 7bc, 8–9
Gospel: Matthew 21:23–27

READ

> Good and upright is the LORD, therefore he shows
> sinners the way, He guides the humble in righteous-
> ness, and teaches the humble his way.
>
> —Psalm 25:8–9

REFLECT

The word *sinners* sounds so harsh, doesn't it? I agree that it can leave a bad taste in your mouth, but I also believe that embracing that title is the first step on the road to humility. When we sin, we choose what we want over what God wants. In a sense, it's a refusal to submit to his supreme authority and infinite knowledge. Sinning is essentially denying that the Lord knows what's best for us. It involves confusing the role of creator and creature. In order to recognize sin and see ourselves as sinners, we must be humble.

By embracing the title of "sinner" (without in any way diminishing our value as children of God), the Bible assures us that the Lord will show us the way, guide us in righteousness, and teach us his way. Since that's really what Advent is all about, making that admission will make this a very good place to meet the Lord today.

RESPOND

Throughout the Bible, a great deal of emphasis is placed on the virtue of humility. And while practicing humility is important throughout the year, it's especially critical during the Advent season. Often mistakenly viewed as thinking less of oneself, humility is actually seeing ourselves as we really are. Those who are humble recognize their sinfulness and weakness. They are aware of the importance of grace and the need for a Savior.

In seeking to become humble, there is no better teacher than Jesus. His words "Take my yoke upon you and learn from me, for I am meek and humble of heart; and you will find rest for yourselves" (Mt 11:29) not only call attention to his practice of humility but also serve as a reminder of his desire to teach us. In addition, the Lord highlights the reward for those who live humbly: rest. For those of us who are looking to find some peace in the midst of this hectic season, that promise is very appealing.

PRAY

Dear Jesus, as I continue my Advent journey, I acknowledge the fact that I am a sinner and that I need you as my Savior. It's not easy for me to admit this, but I know it's necessary. I desire to become humbler, Lord, but I know it can't happen without the help of your grace. Please help me to recognize my weakness and better appreciate your strength. Knowing you're here for me gives me the confidence I need to move forward for the remainder of Advent. With you as my guide, I know I can succeed. Amen.

Tuesday

THIRD WEEK OF ADVENT

Reading: Zephaniah 3:1–2, 9–13
Responsorial Psalm: Psalm 34:2–3, 6–7, 17–18, 19, 23
Gospel: Matthew 21:28–32

READ

> Thus says the LORD: Woe to the city, rebellious and polluted, to the tyrannical city! She hears no voice, accepts no correction; In the LORD she has not trusted, to her God she has not drawn near.
>
> —Zephaniah 3:1–2

REFLECT

I recognize the Old Testament harshness of today's passage, but the message is too good not to share. Speaking to Jerusalem, the prophet Zephaniah lets the people know why the Lord appears to be absent. With incredible bluntness, he reminds them that the fault lies with them.

Regardless of what I do or don't do to prepare, Advent will end on December 25. If I haven't made extra room in my life for Jesus between now and then, my relationship with him will not grow. If that happens (and I pray it won't), it's entirely my fault. Zephaniah's words shook me up when I read them, but in a good way. His message motivates me to make the most of the remaining days of Advent. If I do my part, I know Jesus will do his part.

RESPOND

At a time when we're surrounded with messages of peace and hope, the "fire and brimstone" preaching found in today's first reading stands out like a sore thumb. Even though we might prefer a more feel-good message, these words can be highly motivational and fit in nicely with the goal of Advent.

While it's true that the Holy Spirit is ultimately responsible for our Advent progress, we do have a part to play. Drawing closer to the Lord does involve work on our part. The fact that you're reading this serves as proof that you're trying to prepare to celebrate the arrival of Jesus in a few weeks with a full heart, but it can't stop there. In addition to reading these reflections and the associated scripture passages, we need to make sure we're applying them to our lives. Readings like this remind us that sometimes we don't want to hear what God has to say. But for our Advent preparation to bear good fruit, we need to trust the Lord, listen to his words, and accept correction when needed. It all comes down to humility and obedience. It's a great reminder as we head toward the finish line.

In the days to come, let's do our best to approach the daily scripture readings with an open mind. We'll take comfort in messages of hope, accept the call to change our ways, and pray for the grace to hear the Lord's voice. Doing that will ensure that this Advent will bear good fruit.

PRAY

Dear Jesus, I'm grateful for this much-needed reminder from the Old Testament today. I may have wasted some opportunities during the first two weeks of Advent, but I know it's not too late. This year, I still want to grow closer to you than ever before. Please open my mind to recognize my problem areas and grant me the grace to make the necessary changes. Thanks for being so patient with me. I really appreciate it. Amen.

Wednesday
THIRD WEEK OF ADVENT

Reading: Isaiah 45:6c–8, 18, 21c–25
Responsorial Psalm: Psalm 85:9ab, 10, 11–12, 13–14
Gospel: Luke 7:18b–23

READ

> John summoned two of his disciples and sent them to the Lord to ask, "Are you the one who is to come, or should we look for another?"
>
> —Luke 7:18

REFLECT

John the Baptist gets a great deal of attention during Advent, but we're definitely not used to seeing him like this. In the Gospel from today's daily Mass, John appears to be questioning the role of Jesus as Messiah. Confined to a prison cell, John summoned two of his disciples and instructed them to ask Jesus if he was indeed "the one who is to come."

Choosing to avoid a direct answer, Jesus instructed the messengers to tell John what they have seen and heard: "The blind regain their sight, the lame walk, lepers are cleansed, the deaf hear, the dead are raised, the poor have the good news proclaimed to them" (Lk 7:22). Instead of answering the question directly, Jesus called attention to all of his Messianic deeds. By doing this, his "non-answer" was arguably more effective than a simple yes or no. After all, anyone could claim to be the "one who is to come," but only the true Messiah could perform the miraculous works associated with his ministry.

Over the years, John the Baptist's motivation for sending his followers to Jesus has been debated. Some speculate that he did it to satisfy his own doubts, while others believe he did it to benefit his disciples. While it's certainly valid to reflect on John's reasoning, let's momentarily put aside that question and assume that the question and answer are for *our* benefit. In other words, let's assume *we* are the disciples John is sending to Jesus. We asked Jesus the question, and we heard his answer. Now what?

RESPOND

By putting ourselves in the position of those questioning Jesus ("Are you the one who is to come, or should we look for another?"), we're forced to consider an uncomfortable but necessary question: is Jesus really who he claims to be? Don't feel bad about asking that question. Jesus not only wants you to ask it but also wants to answer it. As we prepare to surrender our lives more fully to him during this season, we should use the time to get to know him as a person and not just an idea or historical figure.

So how can we be sure that Jesus is the "real deal" and not just a figment of our imagination? While it's true that we have to rely on faith, there are a few things we can do to strengthen our belief. For starters, I recommend you look at the answer Jesus gave to John's disciples. The Lord's actions definitely support his messianic claims. Next, read through the first chapter of Mark's gospel (add chapter 2 if you're feeling inspired!) and reflect on Jesus's mighty deeds. In the following prayer, we'll ask the Holy Spirit to strengthen our belief that Jesus Christ is truly the Messiah and worthy of our trust.

PRAY

Dear Jesus, thank you for allowing me to eavesdrop on your conversation with John's disciples. By pointing to your miraculous deeds, you offer concrete proof that you are the Messiah. Because I know you want me to really and truly believe in you, I ask you to awaken your Holy Spirit in me and allow the scriptures to penetrate my heart. You understand that words aren't enough, and that's why you give me the gift of faith through the working of your Spirit. I believe in my head, Lord. Now, I ask you to let me believe in my heart and with my life. Amen.

Thursday
THIRD WEEK OF ADVENT

Reading: Isaiah 54:1–10
Responsorial Psalm: Psalm 30:2, 4, 5–6, 11–12a, 13b
Gospel: Luke 7:24–30

READ

> Enlarge the space for your tent, spread out your tent
> cloths unsparingly; lengthen your ropes and make
> firm your pegs.
>
> —Isaiah 54:2

REFLECT

As someone who lives in a small house, I understand the importance of avoiding clutter. Ever since my family took the major step of downsizing, we have lived by a simple rule: before something large comes into the house, there must be a place for it. Typically, a decision must be made and something has to go.

We can apply the same lesson to our lives, especially when it comes to spiritual matters. That's why, during the Advent season, the Church encourages us to remove some of the clutter that fills our lives and free up room for Jesus. If we make room for the Lord, he will gladly occupy the space.

In the first reading from today's daily Mass, however, the prophet Isaiah takes that concept to the next level. In anticipation of the coming of the Messiah, he encourages the people to not only clean up their existing space but also spread out and acquire additional space for the Lord.

It's not always intentional, but we often create boundaries for God. We'll worship him on Sunday or serve him to a point, but that's it. This verse challenges us to go beyond fitting him into our current schedule and encourages us to make additional room for him.

RESPOND

Why should we be content to free up a little space for Jesus during Advent? Instead of just carving out some extra prayer time or making an effort to encounter him more deeply at church, let's make room for him in every area of our lives. If you invite Jesus into your workplace, school, or personal life, I guarantee he's going to show up. Once that happens, you'll finally find the peace you've been seeking.

One thing to keep in mind is the fact that Jesus wants to be involved in your life. He didn't come to our world to sit in the synagogue all day. Examining his life in the gospels provides ample evidence that he was always seeking out those he came to save, even when he was tired. Jesus was the ultimate people person! As a result, you can rest assured that he is anxiously awaiting for your invitation.

While this entire book is part of the process, the following prayer will let Jesus know that you want him to occupy a bigger part of your life. We'll leave the details up to him. Today, just invite him to get involved in every area of your life—and expect him to respond. More than just pious words, this prayer is a sincere request expressed to someone who has the ability to give you greater peace than you could ever imagine.

PRAY

Dear Jesus, this Advent, I'm not content to just meet you in church. Instead, I invite you to occupy all areas of my life. You are welcome in my home, workplace, and personal life. I'd like you to help me with all my concerns and worries. Thank you for your willingness to get involved in the messiness of my life. I know it will make a big difference. Amen.

Friday
THIRD WEEK OF ADVENT

Reading: Isaiah 56:1–3a, 6–8
Responsorial Psalm: Psalm 67:2–3, 5, 7–8
Gospel: John 5:33–36

READ

> John was a burning and shining lamp, and for a
> while you were content to rejoice in his light. But I
> have testimony greater than John's.
>
> —John 5:35–36

REFLECT

Because John the Baptist had an attractive and hope-filled message, it's easy to see why his disciples were content with following him. Even though they may have heard the news about Jesus, why should they fix what isn't broken? John's disciples were likely comfortable and feeling good about following God's will—they probably had no idea what a relationship with Jesus could bring.

Once Jesus came on the scene, John's ministry became obsolete, and he knew it. As a result, he let his disciples know that he wasn't "the one." Apparently, however, John's words weren't enough to get the job done. Knowing their leader was a "burning and shining lamp," his followers were reluctant to leave. To get John's followers moving, Jesus had to speak out by promising that he had a "testimony greater than John's."

I can understand the way they thought. Before I became a full-time author and speaker, I worked in the software industry for thirty years. During that time, I worked for only three companies. It took a lot for me to change jobs. Even when I wasn't happy with my current position, I was hesitant to make a move because the new job might be even worse. Contentment can lead to complacency, which is never a good thing. John's disciples may have had a good thing, but God had something better in mind for them. Jesus was now on the scene, and it was time to make a move.

RESPOND

It's easy to become content in our relationship with Jesus, but it's generally not a good idea. Even though I like to be totally in control of my spiritual journey, I recognize that it's better to yield to the Holy Spirit. He knows what I need better than I do. For the remainder of Advent, let's try to be more accepting of those unexpected interruptions and our lack of spiritual progress. To grow closer to Jesus, we should be willing to move beyond contentment and follow the lead of his Spirit.

We may have a general idea, but none of us know exactly what we need during Advent. Fortunately, the Holy Spirit knows exactly what we need. And just like the disciples of John the Baptist, we might need to be stretched or moved in a different direction. I may be writing this book and designing the daily exercises, but I don't know exactly what you need. We can all stand to grow closer to Jesus in some way, but only the Spirit knows the exact details. In the following prayer, we'll relinquish control and give him permission to take us where we need to go.

PRAY

Dear Jesus, for the remainder of Advent, I ask that you lead me to where I need to be. Like John's disciples, I must be willing to move away from contentment and move closer to you. I know it won't always be easy, so please grant me the grace I need and the courage to follow your lead. Please arrange my circumstances and awaken your Holy Spirit in me as I attempt to grow closer to you during the Advent season. Help me yield to the Spirit instead of trying to control my spiritual progress. If I fail in my efforts, may I always remember that you might be trying to teach me something. You know best, Jesus. I trust you. Amen.

NOTE: There's no Saturday reading because Saturday of the third week of Advent always occurs between December 17 and 24, so from this point on, please see "Weekdays of Advent: December 17–24" starting on page 99 to continue the daily reflections.

The Finish Line Is in Sight!

Fourth Sunday of Advent
YEAR A

First Reading: Isaiah 7:10–14
Responsorial Psalm: Psalm 24:1–2, 3–4, 5–6
Second Reading: Romans 1:1–7
Gospel: Matthew 1:18–24

READ

> Who may go up the mountain of the Lord? Who can stand in his holy place? "The clean of hand and pure of heart, who has not given his soul to useless things, what is vain."
>
> —Psalm 24:3–4

REFLECT

As we enter the final week of Advent, this passage summarizes what we've been trying to do for the past three weeks. Growing closer to the Lord (ascending his mountain or standing in his holy place) involves a joint effort of our desires, heart, and hands. When these three components work in unison, we grow in our capacity for God to make us holy.

Let's discuss each of these three areas, starting with desire. To grow in holiness and invite Jesus more deeply into our lives, we must first desire it. That initial desire is what gets the ball rolling and allows us to reach our goal. It may sound obvious, but unless we want to grow closer to the Lord, it's never going to happen.

Our desire to grow in holiness won't bear fruit unless it's fueled by the heart or will. Pure desire alone is not enough to get us over the finish line. Simply put, there will be days when we don't feel like working at achieving our goal. That's when the will must take over and we resolve to move forward no matter how we feel.

The final piece to look at is our hands, or the work. To climb the mountain of holiness, we must work at it. Even though the Holy Spirit is in charge of the operation, we must cooperate with his grace and do our part.

RESPOND

A fruitful Advent journey involves a combination of desire, will, and work. If placed under the control of the Holy Spirit, these three practices will yield positive results. The good news is that by reaching this part of the book, you're well on your way to your target goal: a closer relationship with Jesus Christ.

Here's some evidence to support my theory. First, you wouldn't have obtained and opened the book without having the desire for a good Advent. Second, I believe it's safe to assume that there was at least one day when you didn't feel like reading the reflection. You did it solely as an act of the will. Finally, by reading and putting into practice these daily reflections, you are working toward the goal of a closer relationship with Jesus. You are on your way to ascending the mountain and standing in his holy place. Keep up the good work. We're almost there!

PRAY

Dear Jesus, thank you for giving us the opportunity to prepare for you during Advent. Please grant me the grace to make the most of the remainder of the season. Increase my desire to change, let me know which areas in my life still need cleaning up, and strengthen my will to do the remaining cleaning. I'm grateful that you're giving me the opportunity to do some spiritual housecleaning, and I look forward to welcoming you more fully into my freshly cleaned life during our Christmas celebration. Amen.

Fourth Sunday of Advent
YEAR B

First Reading: 2 Samuel 7:1–5, 8b–12, 14a, 16
Responsorial Psalm: Psalm 89:2–3, 4–5, 27, 29
Second Reading: Romans 16:25–27
Gospel: Luke 1:26–38

READ

> I will assign a place for my people Israel and I will plant them in it to dwell there; they will never again be disturbed, nor shall the wicked ever again oppress them, as they did at the beginning.
>
> —2 Samuel 7:10

REFLECT

The nation of Israel had many enemies and, as a result, became accustomed to living in a constant state of fear. Their lack of power made them a target for their stronger neighbors. In a world where "might was right," the Israelites were often helpless victims to their oppressors. It was a tough way to live.

With these words, however, the Lord offers them hope for a brighter future. Although they will not see the promise fulfilled immediately, they can take immediate comfort in the fact that they will one day live in peace. One day, the enemies who cause them so much grief will no longer be a threat to them.

We can view our Advent experience in a similar way. Even though we're still journeying, we can rejoice in what will happen in the not-so-distant future. Provided we continue to do our share of the work, we can rest assured that the Lord will hold up his end of the bargain. On Christmas Day, we can count on the fact that the peace of Christ will dwell in our hearts more than it did at the beginning of Advent.

RESPOND

I believe the best way to respond to the Lord's promise is by thanking him for the peace that is headed our way. You have probably experienced a down payment of that peace already, but it's going to get even better. Throughout Advent, these daily reflections have been focused on becoming more aware of our spiritual problem areas and taking the necessary actions to prepare for the coming of Christ. Along with that comes greater peace.

Although every day of Advent is special, Sundays are extra special. Today is the final Sunday before Christmas. Let's make use of the Lord's Day to reflect on where we've been and where we're headed. Like the Israelites, we can look back at our pre-Advent lives and recall the tension and oppression that surrounded us. We can then reflect on the peace and hope that have gradually filled our hearts and look forward to a new life with Jesus. And while this new way of life can seem like glorified positive thinking, it's actually much more. Inviting Christ into your life and surrendering to his will is a whole new way of living. What we're preparing for is real, it is life-changing, and it is offered freely.

PRAY

Dear Jesus, as Christmas draws near, I'm getting excited about the new life I will experience in you. Even though I'm feeling more peace than I did at the beginning of Advent, I know it's going to get even better. Like the people of Israel, I'm grateful that you offered me a new way of life. Please grant me the grace to make the most of the final week of Advent and to look forward with anticipation to the ways our Christmas feast marks all the ways you are present to us. Thank you, Lord. Amen.

Fourth Sunday of Advent
YEAR C

First Reading: Micah 5:1–4a
Responsorial Psalm: Psalm 80:2–3, 15–16, 18–19
Second Reading: Hebrews 10:5–10
Gospel: Luke 1:39–45

READ

> O Shepherd of Israel, lend an ear, you who guide
> Joseph like a flock! Seated upon the cherubim, shine
> forth upon Ephraim, Benjamin, and Manasseh. Stir
> up your power, and come to save us.
>
> —Psalm 80:2–3

REFLECT

Written during a time of military defeat, these words express a
hopeful cry for help. As we read these opening words of Psalm
80, a feeling of confident expectation begins to emerge. This plea
is addressed to a powerful God by one who fully expects to be
saved from the enemy.

I find it interesting that this prayer is addressed to the
"Shepherd of Israel," as opposed to "Lord" or "God." Because
the Israelites were very familiar with the relationship between
the shepherd and his sheep, this title is extremely significant. By
their nature, sheep are helpless and totally dependent on their
shepherd. Conversely, the shepherd is the guardian of his flock
and has the power to protect them. The fact that the psalmist

chose this title reveals a healthy understanding of the relationship between the creatures and their creator. They are helpless without him, and they know it.

The final piece of this passage contains a direct plea to the powerful God who can save them. As we celebrate the final Sunday before Christmas, we're invited to make these words our own. We cannot save ourselves or break free from the burden of anxiety and hopelessness. Therefore, we cry out to the Messiah who is about to enter more deeply into our lives.

RESPOND

Looking at this cry from the Israelites gives us good insight into their beliefs. They know they're in trouble and need the Lord's help. By using the "shepherd" title, they're also aware that he cares about them. That understanding flows outward into this prayer. Today would be a good day for us to think about our own beliefs. Do we really know how much God cares about us and wants to help us? Do we understand that he is all powerful?

Two thousand years ago, Jesus came into our world to save us. By taking this radical step, Jesus subjected himself to discomfort, rejection, pain, suffering, and even death. It was the response of a shepherd coming to the assistance of his helpless sheep. It was done not out of a sense of duty but out of love. Specifically, Jesus came into the world because he loves you. If that's the only lesson you get out of today's reflection, it is enough. As we head into the final week of Advent, let's cry out to Jesus in anticipation of his arrival. Come, Lord Jesus!

PRAY

Dear Jesus, I need you to come to my aid. With so many problems and dangers all around me, I feel like a helpless sheep in need of a shepherd. Fortunately, however, this psalm reminds me that you're exactly the right person for the job. As I enter into the final week of Advent, please help me increase my awareness of your love for me and your ability to help. Thank you, Lord. Amen.

REFLECTION FOR DECEMBER 8

Solemnity of the Immaculate Conception of the Blessed Virgin Mary

First Reading: Genesis 3:9–15, 20
Responsorial Psalm: Psalm 98:1, 2–3ab, 3cd–4
Second Reading: Ephesians 1:3–6, 11–12
Gospel: Luke 1:26–38

READ

> Mary said, "Behold, I am the handmaid of the Lord.
> May it be done to me according to your word."
> —Luke 1:38

REFLECT

When the archangel Gabriel traveled to Nazareth and appeared to Mary, he greeted her with the words, "Hail, full of grace! The Lord is with you." His words may sound ordinary to us, but they're actually very profound. For one thing, he referred to her not by name but by the title "full of grace." In the original Greek, this salutation implies her being filled with grace from the time of her conception and provides the basis for the Church's doctrine that she was conceived without the stain of original sin.

Second, let's look at the second part of Gabriel's greeting: "The Lord is with you." In the Old Testament, this greeting was reserved for those individuals chosen by God for a very special mission. Some examples are Joshua (Jos 1:9), the people of Israel (Is 41:10), and Moses (Ex 3:12)—and now Mary. Is it any wonder that Gabriel's greeting would cause this humble virgin from Nazareth to be "greatly troubled"?

Nevertheless, after asking one question ("How can this be, since I have no relations with a man?") and receiving a direct but rather implausible answer ("The Holy Spirit will come upon you, and the power of the Most High will overshadow you"), Mary responded with an unqualified yes.

RESPOND

Today, the Church celebrates the Immaculate Conception of the Blessed Virgin Mary. In addition to reflecting on the fact that she was conceived without original sin, today would be a good day to recognize Mary's incredible faith. Despite the lack of details and the potential difficulties she would face, Mary willingly assented to her God-given mission.

While Mary's faith is definitely praiseworthy, we shouldn't let it stop there. Don't make the mistake of viewing her level of trust as unattainable. Rather, let it motivate you to grow in faith. We may never reach Mary's level of faith, but we can certainly get closer than we are now.

As we continue our Advent journey, let's aim for a more Mary-like faith. And because that may be a little intimidating, it would be a good idea to ask for help by praying the prayer below. While I have intentionally addressed the prayers in this book to Jesus, I don't think he would mind if we depart from that format for one day. On this day, a solemnity dedicated to the Blessed Virgin Mary, let's address our prayer to the Lord's mother. Although she's not divine, the Church recognizes her as the most powerful human intercessor in history. We'll present our prayer to Mary with confidence and believe that, just as she did at the wedding in Cana, she'll present our needs to Jesus.

PRAY

Dear Blessed Mother, thank you for saying yes and delivering our Savior. Your trust in God is amazing. I'd like to be able to trust him as much as you did, and I could really use your help. Please pray for me so that, by the time Christmas rolls around, I will trust him more than I do today. Thank you, Mary. Amen.

December 17–24

December 17

Reading: Genesis 49:2, 8–10
Responsorial Psalm: Psalm 72:1–2, 3–4ab, 7–8, 17
Gospel: Matthew 1:1–17

READ

> The book of the genealogy of Jesus Christ, the son of David, the son of Abraham. Abraham became the father of Isaac, Isaac the father of Jacob, Jacob the father of Judah and his brothers.
>
> —Matthew 1:1–2

REFLECT

The Gospel from today's Mass details the genealogy of Jesus Christ. While it only takes a few minutes to read through these seventeen verses, the actual story took approximately two thousand years to play out. Even though the world was in desperate need of a Savior, the process took place minute by minute, hour by hour, day by day, and year by year.

The Old Testament offers proof that, for thousands of years, God's people were waiting and praying for the arrival of the Messiah. That's a long time to wait for a request that we know God wants to grant and for which there exists an urgent need. As we read through the long list of unusual and often obscure names contained in Matthew's genealogy, we can easily begin to question the Lord's approach. Why did this process take so long and involve so many people?

Aside from teaching us the valuable lesson that the Lord works in mysterious ways, the genealogy of Jesus Christ teaches us that God operates according to his own schedule. Applying this lesson to our own lives may not always make us feel better, but it can give us a greater sense of peace. Sometimes it's frustrating, but God really does know best. If something is God's will, it will occur when the time is right.

RESPOND

The first application of this important, but difficult, lesson involves our Advent preparation. As we look forward to celebrating the Lord's arrival on Christmas Day, we may begin to grow impatient with the process. Why is it necessary to wait, and why must we work so hard at preparing? We know that Jesus wants to become more deeply involved in our lives, so why doesn't it just happen now?

In a similar way to the time when Jesus was born into our world, the process of him entering more fully into our lives involves human cooperation. Just like the men and women whose lives are listed in Matthew's genealogy, we have a role to play in the process. Even if we don't fully comprehend why God chooses to involve us in carrying out his will, we can at least understand that he does.

In addition to helping us better grasp the necessity for Advent preparation, the long and complex genealogy of Jesus Christ can teach us another important life lesson. Many times our prayers seem to go unanswered for long periods. Sometimes, after beginning to pray for a resolution, our circumstances appear to get worse. Looking at the process of sending the Messiah can help us to see that God has his own timetable, which often differs from ours. Let's work on accepting that today.

PRAY

Dear Jesus, it's difficult for me to understand why it took so long for you to come into the world. If it was up to me, I would have moved faster and used a less complicated approach. But because you are God and I am not, I'm going to choose to trust that you arrived in the right way at the right time. Help me to be more willing to trust you and patiently wait for your answers to my prayers. I ask this in your mighty name. Amen.

December 18

Reading: Jeremiah 23:5–8
Responsorial Psalm: Psalm 72:1–2, 12–13, 18–19
Gospel: Matthew 1:18–25

READ

> See, days are coming . . . when I will raise up a righteous branch for David; As king he shall reign and govern wisely, he shall do what is just and right in the land.
>
> —Jeremiah 23:5

REFLECT

You don't have to be a scripture scholar to get a sense of the hope promised by this Bible verse. The people who first heard this proclamation didn't know when the promised king would arrive, but they knew he was on his way. That promise filled them with hope and enabled them to move forward. There may have been uncertainty about the "how and when" of the Messiah's arrival, but there was doubt about the "what and who." The long-awaited Savior was definitely on the way.

Even though the original promise has been fulfilled, that same hope experienced by the Israelites is available to us today. As we continue to work our way through these daily reflections, we are moving closer and closer to entering into the mystery of that anticipated event. Like God's Chosen People, we may not know the exact details of how Jesus will operate in our lives, but we know that he will. That day is coming!

In order to experience the hope of God's past promise, however, we need to do some work. That's what we've been doing for the past three weeks and what we'll continue to do until Christmas. Even though we're no longer awaiting the physical birth of the Savior, we can still await his arrival into our lives. That same "righteous shoot" promised by the prophet Jeremiah is on his way. By spending some time each day reflecting on that promise and getting ready for its fulfillment, we'll be ready to reap the benefits associated with the coming of the Messiah.

RESPOND

This Advent is different than any Advent you've ever experienced before. The overall theme, prayers, and readings may be the same, but your circumstances are different. No matter how many times you have invited Jesus into your life in the past, things are different now. You are different, the world around you is different, and your needs are different. No two Advent seasons are ever the same—so we're able to look forward with anticipation to a "new" coming of the Savior.

Today we are one day closer to the coming of Jesus than we were yesterday. Because of that, we can anticipate what's about to take place with increasing hope. The Savior's arrival is near. As we think about that promise and the benefits it will bring, let's take another look at anything that might be standing in the way.

Speaking of the coming Messiah, Jeremiah assures us that "he shall do what is just and right in the land." We don't have to worry about Jesus showing up and making a positive impact in our lives. Our main concern should be making sure that we're prepared to receive him. In the following prayer, we'll ask Jesus to help identify any areas that still need to change.

PRAY

Dear Jesus, please grant me the grace to make the most of the next week. Let me know which areas in my life still need cleaning up, and grant me the strength to do the cleaning. I'm grateful that you're giving me the opportunity to do some spiritual housecleaning, and I look forward to welcoming you more fully into my freshly cleaned life on Christmas Day. Amen.

December 19

Reading: Judges 13:2–7, 24–25a
Responsorial Psalm: Psalm 71:3–4a, 5–6ab, 16–17
Gospel: Luke 1:5–25

READ

And the angel said to him in reply, "I am Gabriel,
who stand before God. I was sent to speak to you
and to announce to you this good news. But now
you will be speechless and unable to talk until the
day these things take place, because you did not
believe my words, which will be fulfilled at their
proper time."

—Luke 1:19–20

REFLECT

In the Gospel from today's Mass, a heightened sense of expectation begins to build. We have previously looked at various
messianic prophecies, but now his arrival is imminent. Looking
back at Gabriel's appearance to Zechariah, we're in the advantageous position of knowing exactly what's happening. Before our
very eyes, in this Bible passage, we witness the announcement
proclaiming the birth of the last of the Old Testament prophets.
John the Baptist, the one who will announce the arrival of the
Savior, is about to be born.

Backing up a few verses, Gabriel's message to Zechariah
contains some very good news. Despite being advanced in years

and childless, Zechariah and Elizabeth were informed that they were going to have a son. Furthermore, the angel delivered the even better news that their son would be "filled with the Holy Spirit even from his mother's womb" and take on the special role of preparing "a people fit for the Lord."

Despite all of this good news, Zechariah still refused to believe. The assurance that it would happen in the future wasn't enough for him. He needed to see the results in order to believe—I've done the same many times. Gabriel ended this encounter by announcing that his words "will be fulfilled at the proper time."

RESPOND

In our prayers in the opening days of Advent, we told Jesus that we wanted to draw closer to him and asked for the grace to remain faithful. Over the past three weeks, we've asked the Lord to identify the areas that needed changing and prayed for the grace to turn toward him. While not directly mentioning it every day, that's a good, general overview of what we've been working on for the past three weeks.

Even though we've been working on it every day, you might not be feeling much different from when we started this journey. Are you willing to keep moving forward, choosing to believe the Lord's promise that those who ask *will* receive and those who seek *will* find?

In the end, faith isn't about seeing. It's about choosing to believe. Sometimes we have to believe before we can see. Zechariah had a difficult time believing that all things are possible for God. Despite his priestly role, he couldn't get past his personal beliefs and feelings. What Gabriel promised just didn't make sense to him.

Today, I recommend that we rise above what we may be feeling and *choose to believe* that our Advent preparation will make a difference, and that we'll end up being closer to Jesus on Christmas Day than we were on the first day of Advent.

PRAY

Dear Jesus, you assured us that those who ask will receive and those who seek will find. Even though Advent is almost over and I don't feel much different, I believe you will meet me in my desire to grow closer to you. Thank you for your faithfulness, Lord. I'm looking forward to welcoming you into my life more deeply and celebrating the fullness of your love for us at Christmas. Amen.

December 20

Reading: Isaiah 7:10–14
Responsorial Psalm: Psalm 24:1–2, 3–4ab, 5–6
Gospel: Luke 1:26–38

READ

> Then the angel said to her, "Do not be afraid, Mary,
> for you have found favor with God."
>
> —Luke 1:30

REFLECT

It's hardly a secret that the archangel Gabriel was sent by God to Nazareth in Galilee to speak to a virgin named Mary. As we approach Christmas Day, you'll likely hear this story mentioned several times, and rightfully so. With this visit, God's plan to redeem the world shifted into high gear. The Word of God was becoming flesh—that's a big deal!

What isn't typically emphasized, however, is Mary's reaction to the angel's greeting. The Bible tells us that she was "greatly troubled at what was said," a point that was specifically addressed by Gabriel. Understandably, with so much else going on, it almost seems inappropriate to focus on Mary's fear. While I do understand that line of thinking, I believe her fear is an important detail we should address.

Why is it so important to recognize that Mary was afraid? For one thing, it reminds us that being afraid is not a sin. Fear is an emotion that, according to the teaching of the Church, is neither right nor wrong. The fact that Mary, who was conceived without original sin, experienced the feeling of fear certainly takes the pressure off of us. What matters most is not how we feel but how we respond to our feelings. Mary may have been afraid, but she pushed past her fear and embraced her mission with total trust in God. That step of faith is a sign of her virtue and worthy of our attention.

RESPOND

Even though we may want to eliminate fear from our lives, it actually serves a purpose. Fear is a God-given emotion designed to alert us to potential danger. Once we recognize the feeling of fear, we can then take appropriate action to remove ourselves from danger.

While we do know that Mary's fear was triggered by Gabriel's initial greeting (Lk 1:29), we can only speculate on what specifically troubled her. We touched on this in our reflection on December 8, but it's worth revisiting. Mary's fear may have been a humble person's reaction to being praised by an angel, or it may have been the trepidation caused by receiving the familiar Old Testament reassurance that "the Lord is with you," a greeting ordinarily reserved for those selected for an important mission. We may not know the exact cause of Mary's fear, but we do know that it didn't stop her from doing God's will. Let's allow that to be our goal today. In the following prayer, we'll ask for the grace to respond to fear with a Mary-like trust in God.

PRAY

Dear Jesus, even though I'm feeling afraid today, I choose to trust that you know what's best for me. Please grant me the grace to be more like Mary and surrender to your will. I realize that trusting you is a choice and not a feeling. Through the intercession of the Blessed Mother, I ask that you strengthen my faith so that I don't give in to my fears. Amen.

December 21

Reading: Song of Songs 2:8–14 or Zephaniah 3:14–18a
Responsorial Psalm: Psalm 33:2–3, 11–12, 20–21
Gospel: Luke 1:39–45

READ

> Blessed are you who believed that what was spoken
> to you by the Lord would be fulfilled.
>
> —Luke 1:45

REFLECT

Yesterday, we looked at the fear Mary experienced when visited by the archangel Gabriel. While it's important to recognize that even the immaculately conceived Mary experienced the emotion of fear, it's even more important to emphasize that her fear was in no way connected with doubt. After giving her consent, Mary fully believed that God's unusual plan would fall into place. Even though the details revealed by the angel were bizarre (to say the least), her faith in God didn't waver. Mary believed.

From time to time, I'll hear a theory that Mary was afraid because of what the future might hold. As we discussed previously, the Bible blows that theory to smithereens. Luke clearly states that Mary was greatly troubled by Gabriel's greeting (Lk 1:29) and not because of any future concerns. Any other theory is purely speculative and contradicted by scripture.

Another opinion that's sometimes expressed is that Mary doubted God's plan. Typically centered on her question in Luke

1:34 ("How can this be, since I have no husband?" [RSVCE]), some believe that Mary doubted the angel's words. Apparently, Gabriel didn't think so because he simply answered her question by providing some general details of how the plan would unfold. While this can be used to refute the "doubt" theory, the words we read today from Elizabeth conclusively put it to rest. Filled with the Holy Spirit (Lk 1:41), Elizabeth recognized and power-fully proclaimed that Mary believed what was spoken to her by the Lord would be fulfilled. Mary did not doubt. She believed.

RESPOND

Based on yesterday's reflection and the teaching of the Church, we can safely conclude that it's not a sin to be afraid. While Mary's fear was clearly documented in the Bible, the Catholic Church has declared her to be free from any original or actual sin. Fear is an emotion or feeling and is not sinful in any way.

With that in mind, fear that leads to inaction or deliberate doubt is another story. If we believe something is God's will and we fail to act or give in to serious doubt, we're on shaky spiritual ground. Even if it's not always sinful, hesitation or deliberate doubt caused by fear is something we want to work on. Mary's ability to move from fear to faith gives us hope that it can be done.

As we continue our journey through the final days of Advent, let's once again turn to ask for Mary's help. As we did on the Solemnity of the Immaculate Conception, let's beg our heavenly Mother to go to Jesus and obtain for us some of the graces that enabled her to believe in God's providence even though she was afraid. I know she'll be happy to do so.

PRAY

Dear Blessed Mother, thank you for giving me such a great example of faith. You never doubted that God's plan would be fulfilled. Please ask Jesus to grant me the grace to believe as you believed. Although I have a long way to go, I believe it's possible if you help me. Please help me. Thank you, Mary. Amen.

December 22

Reading: 1 Samuel 1:24–28
Responsorial Psalm: 1 Samuel 2:1, 4–5, 6–7, 8abcd
Gospel: Luke 1:46–56

READ

> The Mighty One has done great things for me.
>
> —Luke 1:49

REFLECT

As we continue to count down the days until Christmas, the Church once again invites us to contemplate the virtues of the Blessed Virgin Mary. In today's Gospel, we hear Mary's response to Elizabeth's praise. Replying to the words of her relative, Mary redirected the praise to the Lord. Using the familiar words of the prayer now known as the Magnificat, she began by proclaiming, "My soul proclaims the greatness of the Lord." While Mary undoubtedly knew she was blessed, she recognized the source of her blessing.

By offering this spoken prayer of gratitude, Mary gives us a glimpse of how she believed. She was humble enough to acknowledge that any greatness or blessedness she possessed could be attributed to God's grace. As we read through the words of her prayer, we see expressions of humility, gratitude, and hope. Above all, we see the words of an individual who is grateful for the goodness and favor of the Lord.

Today's Gospel contains so many great verses that it was difficult to choose just one. I decided to focus on Mary's acknowledgment of God's goodness because it's something we should all recognize. As we prepare to commemorate the birth of Jesus and his arrival into our lives, it seems only appropriate to recognize the "great thing" he has done and is about to do for each of us.

RESPOND

No matter what challenges we're facing, God has done great things for each of us. Not only did he create us out of nothing, but also he has provided for all of our needs from the time we were conceived. Furthermore, he sent his Son to redeem us and make it possible for us to live forever in heaven. Thinking more about his goodness and less about our problems will help us to find the peace we seek. Let's not let it end there, however.

In response to the Lord's goodness to us, let's send up a special prayer of thanksgiving and acknowledgment for all he has done. Rather than compose our own prayer, I suggest we let our Blessed Mother provide the words. After all, she undoubtedly understood God's goodness more than we ever could. Today, let's turn to the Bible and make Mary's Magnificat our own prayer.

PRAY

"My soul proclaims the greatness of the Lord; my spirit rejoices in God my savior. For he has looked upon his handmaid's lowliness; behold, from now on will all ages call me blessed. The Mighty One has done great things for me, and holy is his name. His mercy is from age to age to those who fear him. He has shown might with his arm, dispersed the arrogant of mind and heart. He has thrown down the rulers from their thrones but lifted up the lowly. The hungry he has filled with good things; the rich he has sent away empty. He has helped Israel his servant, remembering his mercy, according to his promise to our fathers, to Abraham and to his descendants forever" (Lk 1:46–55).

December 23

Reading: Malachi 3:1–4, 23–24
Responsorial Psalm: Psalm 25:4–5ab, 8–9, 10, 14
Gospel: Luke 1:57–66

READ

> And the lord whom you seek will come suddenly to
> his temple; The messenger of the covenant whom
> you desire—see, he is coming! says the LORD of
> hosts.
>
> —Malachi 3:1

REFLECT

What I like most about the prophet Malachi's message is the certainty with which he writes. It's apparent that he totally expects the Messiah to arrive. Although he doesn't attempt to predict when the event will occur, he knows it will happen. Let's look closer at some of the important elements of Malachi's prophecy.

The reference to "the lord whom you seek" informs us that the people were actively seeking the Messiah. They weren't simply passing the time twiddling their thumbs. They were deliberately searching for him. This ties in perfectly with Jesus's "seek and you will find" message. During the Lord's time on earth, many people failed to recognize him as the Messiah. Those who desperately seek him are looking, looking, and looking again: "Could he be the one? He's not what I expected, but maybe it's him." The more effort we put into seeking Jesus, the greater our chances are of finding him.

Malachi emphasizes that the Messiah will come suddenly. Because nobody knew for sure when Jesus would arrive, a sudden entrance was guaranteed. Consider the minute before his birth. The world was in darkness, awaiting the Savior's birth. One minute later, everything changed as the Light of the World was born. It doesn't get much more sudden than that!

Along with the fact that the people are actively seeking the Messiah, Malachi calls attention to their desire. They wanted him to arrive and were getting ready to welcome him. Recognizing their desire and that they were actively searching for him, Malachi boldly and emphatically assured them with the following words:

He is coming!

RESPOND

If you've been making room for Jesus over the past four weeks, he will occupy the free space in your life. If not, don't panic. You still have another day to work on it—and the Christmas season extends beyond that. He wants to get involved in your daily life and deliver the peace that only he can give. All you have to do is make room in your life for him.

As today is December 23, this message is especially appropriate. Even though we know Jesus is on his way, we might not be feeling any different. That's totally okay. We will remember and celebrate his "official" arrival day in two more days. The prophecy from Malachi assures us that his arrival will come suddenly, a fact that hasn't changed.

The best way to occupy the remaining two days of Advent is to keep preparing for the Lord's arrival with anticipation and desire. You've made it this far, which is great. Let's keep going for a few more days. If we seek him, we will find him. That's something we can definitely count on.

PRAY

Dear Jesus, it's hard to believe you love me so much that you want to share in the messiness of my life, but I'm glad you do. I could really use your help in these last few days of Advent. Just like those waiting in Malachi's time, I desire for you to get more involved in my life and I'll continue to work at getting ready for you. Please make me aware of any last-minute changes I need to make and grant me the grace to take the necessary action. Thank you, Lord. Amen.

December 24

Reading: 2 Samuel 7:1–5, 8b–12, 14a, 16
Responsorial Psalm: Psalm 89:2–3, 4–5, 27, 29
Gospel: Luke 1:67–79

READ

> In the tender compassion of our God the dawn
> from on high shall break upon us, to shine on those
> who dwell in darkness and the shadow of death, and
> to guide our feet into the way of peace.
> —Luke 1:78–79, NAB

REFLECT

These words, spoken by Zechariah after his speech was restored, remind us of the significance of Christmas. Speaking in the future tense, he recognizes that God's "tender compassion" will result in a wonderful event. The "dawn from on high" shall break upon those "who dwell in darkness and the shadow of death." This event will guide their feet as they receive peace.

When these words were first spoken, the birth of Christ was imminent. That being the case, however, Zechariah took the approach of previous prophets and didn't specify an exact date. Whether he realized it or not, doing so kept the focus on what really mattered. The Messiah was coming. Whether he comes today, tomorrow, or at some point in the future doesn't matter. What does matter is that his arrival will cast light on the darkness and deliver peace to those dwelling in the "shadow of death."

Before we move on, let's reflect on why this great event was going to happen. The sending of the Messiah was taking place because of God's "tender compassion." It may have been thousands of years in the making, but it was definitely going to happen. God loved his people too much to abandon them to a fallen world. He needed to get involved in the most intimate and effective way possible—by sending his Son.

RESPOND

As we examine our final Advent Bible passage and prepare to celebrate the big day, we need to examine the significance of Zechariah's prophecy for us today. While it's true that the physical birth of Jesus has already happened, the message applies every bit as much as it did in the past. For that to happen, however, we need to do some work.

One of the biggest challenges we face during Advent is getting excited about an event that technically took place over two thousand years ago. That was one of the goals of this book, and even though we're nearing the end of the Advent season, it's helpful to revisit why we're preparing and why we should be excited by Zechariah's prophecy.

The birth of Jesus involved his entering into the world in a physical way. When the Word became flesh, everything changed. By the time Jesus finished his mission on earth, the gates of heaven were opened and humanity had been redeemed. That entire process began to unfold at the moment of his birth. Even though those waiting for the Messiah might have been looking for a different kind of ruler, they did believe that the one who was coming would change their lives and liberate them from bondage. They were excited because help was on the way.

In a matter of hours, we'll celebrate the arrival of Jesus. Even though he won't be born again this Christmas Day, his "arrival" has the potential to change your life. Jesus doesn't need another birth in a stable to make a big difference in your life. God loves you so much that he is sending his Son to free you from the invisible chains of sin, anxiety, discouragement, and hopelessness. Through Jesus Christ you can find peace and be freed from captivity. That's what we've been preparing for during the past four weeks. Get ready to celebrate as we welcome the Savior!

PRAY

Dear Jesus, as I get ready to celebrate your birth, I recognize that this Christmas is different from all the previous ones I have celebrated. My life is totally different than it was in the past. I have a whole new set of challenges, and I look forward to letting you help me with them. Thank you, Jesus. I look forward to facing the future and whatever it brings with you. I can say this with confidence because I know I'll never be alone. Amen.

The Word Became Flesh!

Vigil Mass

First Reading: Isaiah 62:1–5
Responsorial Psalm: Psalm 89:4–5, 16–17, 27, 29
Second Reading: Acts 13:16–17, 22–25
Gospel: Matthew 1:1–25

READ

No more shall you be called "Forsaken," nor your land called "Desolate," But you shall be called "My Delight is in her, "and your land "Espoused." For the LORD delights in you, and your land shall be espoused.

—Isaiah 62:4

REFLECT

Things are different now for the people of Israel because our Messiah has arrived. God's people are no longer "forsaken" and their land "desolate." The long-awaited day is here. Let the celebration begin!

It's easy to see the benefit of the Lord entering the world. The darkness has been transformed into light. Even though it will take several more years for the Savior's work to bear fruit, the process has now kicked into high gear. Without a doubt, God's people will benefit tremendously from the event we commemorate today. As we look back with two thousand years of hindsight, we can confirm that their enthusiasm was justified.

It's easy to appreciate the excitement of the people in need of a Savior, but we don't ordinarily stop to consider the Lord's excitement. As this verse clearly informs us, however, the people aren't the only ones who are delighted by his arrival. He is delighted because, in a sense, he's closer to them than ever before. Even though God was always close to his people, taking on human flesh made him more accessible to them.

I think it's safe to say that, because of his infinite wisdom and perfect love, God is more excited than anyone on this day. He is thrilled to be where he always wanted to be. In Jesus, he is literally living with his children.

RESPOND

Just as the Israelites waited and prepared for the Messiah, so have you. Throughout this Advent season, you've prepared for this day to arrive. Even though there was waiting and effort involved, you finished the race. Now it's time to enjoy the fruit of your labor. The waiting is over. Jesus has arrived and your preparations have made you ready for him to take on a greater role in your daily life.

Turning to the Old Testament message from the prophet Isaiah, take a minute to reflect on what's being said. Today is a new day, and the possibilities are endless. Your desire to grow closer to Jesus is fulfilled on this day. Because he delights in you, Jesus is excited to get started. The waiting may have been difficult for you, but try to put yourself in his sandals. In his infinite wisdom, Jesus is fully aware of how much we need him. He's been waiting for some of us for many years. No matter where you stand in your relationship with him, take comfort in the fact that you're now closer to him than you were at the start of Advent. And as emphasized in this verse from Isaiah, both of you have reason to be delighted on this day.

PRAY

Dear Jesus, I can't believe the day is finally here for us to fully celebrate the gift of your presence. I've been waiting for this day for a long time. Even though it seems I'm the one who should be delighted, this verse from Isaiah tells me you're delighted too. Wow, Lord! That makes me feel very special. I'm looking forward to the days ahead as we begin to walk together into the future. Thank you, Jesus. I'm grateful and excited that you're here. Amen.

Mass during the Night

First Reading: Isaiah 9:1–6
Responsorial Psalm: Psalm 96:1–2, 2–3, 11–12, 13
Second Reading: Timothy 2:11–14
Gospel: Luke 2:1–14

READ

> The people who walked in darkness have seen a
> great light; Upon those who lived in a land of gloom
> a light has shone.
>
> —Isaiah 9:1

REFLECT

Looking into the future and reflecting on what life will be like
when the Messiah arrives, Isaiah uses the familiar imagery of
light and darkness. Once Jesus is born, things will be different
for those who accept him as their Lord and Savior. The people
who walked in darkness and lived in a land of gloom will now
reside in a world filled with light.

If you've ever tried to walk in the darkness, you know how
difficult it can be. Not only is it difficult, but also it's danger-
ous. Unfortunately, I learned that lesson the hard way. Several
years ago, I played guitar in a wedding band on weekends. After
packing up my equipment and preparing to head home one eve-
ning, I decided to exit through a storage room located behind
the kitchen. It's the way I came in at the beginning of the night,
and it provided the quickest route to my car. Because I knew
where I was going, I didn't feel the need to turn on the lights.

As I learned, however, walking through a storage room in the daylight is much different than walking through it in the dark. Even though I could see the illuminated parking lot through a small window in the exterior door, I couldn't see the flatbed cart that was directly in front of me. With both hands full of equipment, I fell over the cart and smacked my chin on the concrete floor. I ended up with painful cuts on my chin and both legs. Light really does make a difference!

Although Isaiah isn't writing of a literal darkness into light transformation, the same general principle applies. The arrival of Jesus makes it much easier to navigate the challenges and obstacles of life. As the "image of the invisible God" (Col 1:15), he revealed God's attributes and helped the people experience the Father in a totally new way. He does the same for us and is present to us as the risen Lord, bringing light to our own areas of darkness.

RESPOND

Because the Messiah has already arrived, our situation is different from those who lived before he was born. Due to their oppression and hopelessness, they were actively waiting for his arrival. Those of us who live after the actual birth of Christ are faced with a different set of circumstances, but we still need a savior! Isaiah's prophecy anticipated a future generation that had walked in darkness but would see a great light—we are that generation!

You may not feel any different, but your life has changed today. For the past four weeks, you have been preparing to welcome Jesus into your life. Like the people of old, you anticipated his arrival and worked to free up room in your life for him.

Along the way, Jesus has been "moving in" to help free you from the burdens weighing you down. The peace that comes from a closer relationship with him is yours for the asking—and it is worth celebrating in our Christmas feast.

Even though we rejoice in the ways Jesus comes to us, he isn't going to force himself into your life. Things will only change if you let them. By preparing for him through the daily reflections in this book, however, I'm hopeful that you can better appreciate the benefits of walking through life with him. You no longer have to stumble through the darkness, struggling to avoid life's obstacles and burdens. Someone just flipped on the light switch. His name is Jesus, and he's ready to walk with you.

PRAY

Dear Jesus, I'm so used to walking in the darkness that it will take some time to get accustomed to walking in the light. Thank you for your willingness to enter our world. More specifically, thanks for your willingness to enter into *my* world. You are bigger than all the problems that have been weighing me down, and I'm so glad you're willing to help me with them. I can't wait to see where we're heading. Welcome to my life. Amen.

Mass at Dawn

First Reading: Isaiah 62:11–12
Responsorial Psalm: Psalm 97:1, 6, 11–12
Second Reading: Timothy 3:4–7
Gospel: Luke 2:15–20

READ

> When the angels went away from them to heaven, the shepherds said to one another, "Let us go, then, to Bethlehem to see this thing that has taken place, which the Lord has made known to us."
>
> —Luke 2:15

REFLECT

It was just "another night at the office" for a group of shepherds tending their flock in a field near Bethlehem, or so they thought. In an event that caused them great fear, an angel of the Lord appeared and informed them of the Messiah's birth. If this wasn't overwhelming enough, a whole multitude of angels suddenly appeared giving glory to God!

After the angels departed, the shepherds decided to check it out for themselves and departed "in haste" for Bethlehem. When they arrived at the stable, they found Mary, Joseph, and the infant, and shared the message of the angel. All were amazed at what had been told them by the lowly shepherds, but Mary was especially moved. According to Luke, "Mary kept all these things, reflecting on them in her heart" (Lk 2:19). Then the shepherds departed, "glorifying and praising God for all they had heard and seen" (Lk 2:20). The Bible never mentions them again, but it's highly likely that they were no longer the same upon their return. A close encounter with Jesus tends to have that effect.

The first thing I find commendable about the shepherds is their willingness to follow God. They weren't commanded by the angels to leave their flock and travel to Bethlehem. They chose to do so. Once they learned of the good news, they could have remained in the field reveling in their angelic vision. Doing so would have been much easier for them. Not content with taking the easy route, however, they closed up shop and traveled to Bethlehem. Their effort was rewarded, and they were among the first people to see the long-awaited Messiah in the flesh.

There's something else that strikes me about the shepherd's willingness to step out in faith. By doing so, they put themselves in a position to be used by God as his instruments. It was through them that God communicated an important message to Mary and others. What a great honor. And it all happened because they were willing to go the extra mile for God.

RESPOND

As we celebrate the birth of Jesus today, we can look to the shepherds as a source of inspiration. Not content with just hearing about the Good News, they wanted to experience it for themselves. In a sense, that's where we find ourselves now. Throughout Advent, we've been looking forward to what our "new life" with Jesus would be like. Now it's time to pursue and live it!

Obviously, your life isn't going to magically change in one day. Like the shepherds, however, your encounter with Jesus in this special season will empower you to head into the rest of your life "glorifying and praising God for all [you have] heard and seen." Jesus's birth reveals to us that the ordinary can become extraordinary. All it takes is a shepherd-like desire to follow the Lord where he leads.

Before moving on, let's discuss the other characteristic found in the shepherds: a willingness to be used by God as his instrument. As you continue to grow closer to Jesus, your knowledge of him will increase. Like the shepherds, you'll have the opportunity to share the Good News of Jesus with those around you. Don't let the chance pass you by. You'll never know the life-changing power of your words until you share them with others.

PRAY

Dear Jesus, now that you've arrived, I can't wait to explore our relationship. As I read the details about your birth, I feel like one of the shepherds hearing the Good News for the first time! Please help me get to know you better, Lord, and increase my desire to share you with others. Thank you for the privilege of being able to know you personally and for allowing me to be used as your instrument. Amen.

Mass during the Day

First Reading: Isaiah 52:7–10
Responsorial Psalm: Psalm 98:1, 2–3, 3–4, 5–6
Second Reading: Hebrews 1:1–6
Gospel: John 1:1–18

READ

> And the Word became flesh and made his dwelling among us.
>
> —John 1:14

REFLECT

After thousands of years, the long-awaited Messiah arrived—the Word of God "became flesh" to live among his people. The waiting is over . . . or is it?

Before we answer that question, let's look at the enormity of the event. With the birth of Jesus, God entered the world in the most intimate way possible. Not content with being an invisible and mysterious figure, the Lord humbled himself and came to earth as a helpless infant. The thought of that happening is so mind-boggling that it's easy to see why so many people were unable to grasp what was taking place. Even though the arrival of the Messiah was prophesied and anticipated for generations, very few expected it to happen in this manner. The way this monumental event played out is yet another example of God working in mysterious ways. Only he could come up with a plan like this!

Let's now address the waiting issue. Just because the Messiah arrived didn't necessarily mean the waiting was totally over. When Jesus entered the world over two thousand years ago, his mission was just beginning. Because he arrived as an infant, it took time for him to grow to adulthood. Once he launched his public ministry, it then took approximately three years for him to complete his mission of redeeming the world. The Messiah was definitely on the scene, but the process of redemption would take time to unfold. Nevertheless, the birth of Jesus was definitely a cause for rejoicing. God's promise is being fulfilled.

RESPOND

Today is a day for rejoicing. The arrival of Jesus Christ, the long-anticipated Messiah, changes everything for us.

To better appreciate the significance of this day, however, we have to look at his arrival in a particular way. Obviously, the fact that the Word became flesh two thousand years ago in Bethlehem is a game changer, but it's probably not enough to get you overly excited at this moment. To get really excited about the arrival of Jesus, something else is needed. The presence of the Messiah has to become personal. In other words, you must consider that Jesus came into the world to rescue *you*. He is a personal Savior for each of us.

Even if you don't feel any different today, rest assured that any preparatory work you put in during Advent will bear fruit in your life. Jesus will always go where he's welcome. Therefore, your desire to welcome him more deeply into your life will bear fruit. He will occupy any empty space that you carved out for him. Your "new life" with Jesus begins anew every day you open yourself to his presence.

Today is a day to celebrate because Jesus's birth means he is ready to play a bigger part in your life. Just like what was experienced by God's people two thousand years ago, however, your waiting is both over and also not yet over. While we celebrate Jesus's arrival and his radical presence among us, don't expect your life to change instantaneously. The impact will be felt gradually, over the course of your life. Day by day, with the help of Jesus, your life will take on new meaning and you'll experience greater peace. Even though you'll still have trials and concerns, your burden should become lighter and your hope for the future will grow.

PRAY

Dear Jesus, welcome to my day. I'm glad you were born, but I'm even gladder that you're going to play a greater role in my life. Even if I don't feel any different, I believe my life has changed for the better. With your assistance, I expect my challenges to be less burdensome and my cross less heavy. I have looked forward to celebrating this day with you, Lord. Help me to be patient as we head into the future. My goal is to follow you wherever you lead. Thank you for your willingness to help me. Amen.

CONCLUSION

Merry Christmas!

Guess what? It looks as if Christmas arrived before our own personal judgment day (we're still alive!) and before the Second Coming of Jesus. Therefore, we're in that scenario of having prepared to celebrate Christmas Day with full hearts because it signifies the many ways Jesus arrives in the here and now of daily life. What do we do now?

Before going any further, I want to wish you a merry Christmas. I pray the newborn Savior of the world will fill your heart with peace for the rest of your earthly life. The celebration of the Lord's birth is a really big deal. We commemorate an event that has not only immediate consequences but also eternal ones. Even though the actual birth of Jesus took place over two thousand years ago, something happened today that can transform your life and deliver peace the world cannot give. Give yourself time to enjoy it.

Christmas is too great of a blessing to be crammed into one day. For this reason, the Church will continue the celebration for the next few weeks. Our Christmas feast starts with the Octave of Christmas (which runs through January 1) and continues up until the Feast of the Baptism of the Lord. This feast encourages us to remember and celebrate the great occasion when the Word became flesh. Even though much of the world will be starting to take down Christmas decorations on December 26, our celebration is just beginning as Catholics. Allow yourself to enjoy the peace of the newborn Savior for the remainder of this Christmas season.

Now let's examine what happens after the Christmas season is over. Although the official celebration comes to an end, the peace of Christ is still available to each of us. I look at the Christmas season as a time for reflecting on the impact of Jesus entering the world—and as we discussed earlier, not just entering *the* world but entering *my* world. The birth of Jesus is a life-transforming event that continues to change lives year after year. That transformative potential exists for each of us. All that's needed is desire and the willingness to do some work to dispose ourselves to receive that gift.

Let's take a closer look at what I mean by desire and work. Desire doesn't always appear as an urge to get closer to Jesus. It certainly can, but not always. Sometimes it manifests itself as a desire for greater peace and happiness. Those of us who struggle with anxiety and the burdens of life know what that's all about. I've been seeking peace and happiness all of my life, and I know I'm not alone. We all desire peace and happiness in life. In fact, God created us with that desire in our hearts. In reality, however, that longing for peace and happiness is actually a desire for the Lord and can only be truly satisfied through a relationship with him. Therefore, your desire for greater peace and happiness is actually a hunger for Jesus.

What about the work that it takes to receive this peace? If you're like me, the thought of doing extra work sounds intimidating. But don't let the idea frighten you. Here's why. By making it to this point in the book, you've proven you can do the work.

All through Advent, you've worked on your relationship with Jesus, and it took only a few minutes each day. As you probably now realize, "Jesus time" typically results in some degree of increased peace. Continuing the process throughout the year will enable God to become the center of your life, which will bring the peace and happiness you seek.

In a sense, life is like one big Advent season. Each day provides an opportunity to prepare for our ultimate meeting with Jesus. Taking advantage of these daily opportunities will not only help us on judgment day but also allow us to experience peace and comfort in our lives now. It may feel a little selfish to seek something that makes you feel good, but that's not the case at all. Jesus wants you to experience peace and happiness in this life. In fact, that's one of the reasons he died for you on Calvary. By following him and surrendering your will to the will of the Father, you will be able to experience that peace. The fact that the journey sometimes leads to suffering doesn't affect the peace one bit. By following Jesus and working on our relationship with him, we can experience peace and happiness even in the midst of suffering.

Now that Advent is over and this book is about to come to a close, how do we proceed? I have a few suggestions. For one thing, I recommend that you read from the Bible each day. I fully understand that it may sound overwhelming, but it doesn't have to be. There are many daily devotionals that allow you to read and reflect on Bible verses for a few minutes each day. I have written several such books, which you can find on my website FollowingTheTruth.com. Another great way to obtain your daily dose of scripture is through the Mass readings for each day. I've found this to be an excellent, practical way of hearing the Lord's voice daily. You can access these readings online, in a missal, on the US bishops' website (usccb.org), or through a monthly magazine. The resources are readily available and can fit into the busiest of schedules.

In addition to reading the Bible, make a point to spend some time each day conversing with Jesus in prayer. As evidenced by our daily Advent prayers, your conversation can be short and to the point. More than anything else, Jesus desires to spend time with you. He wants you to speak to him from the heart. Don't hold back. Thank him for all he's done for you, but also share your fears and concerns. Let him know you're afraid, tired, or even angry. He loves you unconditionally and won't get offended by anything you say. Also, don't forget to ask for help with your daily struggles. Whether you're trying to overcome a certain sin or looking to find peace, ask Jesus to help you. It is what he was sent to do!

Another great way to get to know Jesus and experience his peace is through the sacraments. The grace that flows from the sacraments is an excellent source of comfort and will greatly enhance your relationship with the Lord. Some sacraments can be received only once (Baptism and Confirmation), but they come with a lifetime supply of grace. All it takes is your desire to tap into that grace. A short prayer, such as "Come, Holy Spirit!" is a great way to release that unlimited grace daily. The other sacraments can be received as needed, depending on your circumstances. Of those other sacraments, the Eucharist and Reconciliation are the ones you will probably receive the most frequently. I strongly encourage you to do so. Although I benefit every day in some way from all the sacraments I've received, those two are my lifeline. I don't always succeed, but

I try my best to receive the Eucharist daily and Reconciliation every two weeks. It has truly been life changing. Even though I don't always *feel* any different afterward, I believe by faith that they do change me; looking back in hindsight, I can see that the sacraments make a big difference in my life. Please take advantage of them. You won't regret it.

Thank you for walking through Advent with me. I'm confident that if you keep doing what you've done over the past four weeks, your relationship with Jesus will continue to grow and so will your peace. As we've discussed previously, he desires that relationship even more than you do. Keep on asking, seeking, and knocking. Your efforts will be fruitful. You are in my daily prayers.

> Ask and it will be given to you; seek and you will find; knock and the door will be opened to you. For everyone who asks, receives; and the one who seeks, finds; and to the one who knocks, the door will be opened. (Mt 7:7–8)

Gary Zimak is a Catholic speaker and the bestselling author of several books, including *Give Up Worry for Lent!*, *Let Go of Anger and Stress!*, *Give Up Worry for Good!*, *Let Go of Your Fear*, and *When Your Days Are Dark, God is Still Good.*

He is the host of *The Gary Zimak Show* and the podcast *Following the Truth.* He previously served as director of parish services at Mary, Mother of the Redeemer Catholic Church in North Wales, Pennsylvania, and as the host of *Spirit in the Morning* on Holy Spirit Radio in Philadelphia, Pennsylvania. He is a frequent speaker and retreat leader at Catholic parishes and conferences across the country.

His work has appeared in *Catholic Digest, National Catholic Register, Catholic Exchange, Catholic Philly*, and *Catholic Answers Magazine.* Zimak has been a guest on numerous television and radio programs, including EWTN's *Bookmark* and *Women of Grace, Catholic Answers Live, Morning Air*, and the *Son Rise Morning Show.*

Zimak earned a bachelor of science degree in business administration from Drexel University.

He lives in Mount Laurel, New Jersey, with his wife. They have two children.

www.followingthetruth.com
Facebook: Gary.Zimak.speaker.author
Twitter: @gary_zimak